The right to die,
179.7 Fer

Ferguson, John E.

D0070619

The Right to Die

POINT // // // /
\\\\\\\\\ COUNTERPOINT

Affirmative Action
Amateur Athletics
American Military Policy
Animal Rights
Capital Punishment
DNA Evidence
Educational Standards
Election Reform
The FCC and Regulating Indecency
Fetal Rights
Freedom of Speech
Gay Rights
Gun Control
Immigrants' Rights After 9/11
Immigration Policy
Legalizing Marijuana
Mandatory Military Service
Media Bias
Mental Health Reform
Miranda Rights
Open Government
Physician-Assisted Suicide
Policing the Internet
Prisoners' Rights
Private Property Rights
Protecting Ideas
Religion in Public Schools
The Right to Die
The Right to Privacy
Rights of Students
Search and Seizure
Smoking Bans
Stem Cell Research and Cloning
Tort Reform
Trial of Juveniles as Adults
The War on Terror
Welfare Reform
Women in the Military

The Right to Die

John E. Ferguson Jr., J.D.

SERIES CONSULTING EDITOR
Alan Marzilli, M.A., J.D.

CHELSEA HOUSE
P U B L I S H E R S
An imprint of Infobase Publishing

The Right to Die

Chelsea House
An imprint of Infobase Publishing
132 West 31st Street
New York NY 10001

Library of Congress Cataloging-in-Publication Data

Ferguson, John E.
  The Right to die / John E. Ferguson, Jr.
    p. cm. — (Point/counterpoint)
  Includes bibliographical references and index.
  ISBN-13: 978-0-7910-9287-3 (hardcover)
  ISBN-10: 0-7910-9287-9 (hardcover)
  1. Right to die—Juvenile literature. 2. Euthanasia—Juvenile literature.
  3. Assisted suicide—Juvenile literature. 4. Medical ethics—Juvenile literature.
  I. Title. II. Series.

  R726.F39 2007
  179.7--dc22   2007003653

Chelsea House books are available at special discounts when purchased in bulk quantities for businesses, associations, institutions, or sales promotions. Please call our Special Sales Department in New York at (212) 967-8800 or (800) 322-8755.

You can find Chelsea House on the World Wide Web at
  http://www.chelseahouse.com

Series design by Keith Trego
Cover design by Ben Peterson

Printed in the United States of America

Bang NSMG 10 9 8 7 6 5 4 3 2 1

This book is printed on acid-free paper.

All links and Web addresses were checked and verified to be correct at the time of publication. Because of the dynamic nature of the Web, some addresses and links may have changed since publication and may no longer be valid.

CONTENTS

Foreword

Alan Marzilli, M.A., J.D.
Washington, D.C.

The debates presented in POINT/COUNTERPOINT are among the most interesting and controversial in contemporary American society, but studying them is more than an academic activity. They affect every citizen; they are the issues that today's leaders debate and tomorrow's will decide. The reader may one day play a central role in resolving them.

Why study both sides of the debate? It's possible that the reader will not yet have formed any opinion at all on the subject of this volume—but this is unlikely. It is more likely that the reader will already hold an opinion, probably a strong one, and very probably one formed without full exposure to the arguments of the other side. It is rare to hear an argument presented in a balanced way, and it is easy to form an opinion on too little information; these books will help to fill in the informational gaps that can never be avoided. More important, though, is the practical function of the series: Skillful argumentation requires a thorough knowledge of *both* sides—though there are seldom only two, and only by knowing what an opponent is likely to assert can one form an articulate response.

Perhaps more important is that listening to the other side sometimes helps one to see an opponent's arguments in a more human way. For example, Sister Helen Prejean, one of the nation's most visible opponents of capital punishment, has been deeply affected by her interactions with the families of murder victims. Seeing the families' grief and pain, she understands much better why people support the death penalty, and she is able to carry out her advocacy with a greater sensitivity to the needs and beliefs of those who do not agree with her. Her relativism, in turn, lends credibility to her work. Dismissing the other side of the argument as totally without merit can be too easy—it is far more useful to understand the nature of the controversy and the reasons *why* the issue defies resolution.

The most controversial issues of all are often those that center on a constitutional right. The Bill of Rights—the first ten amendments to the U.S. Constitution—spells out some of the most fundamental rights that distinguish the governmental system of the United States from those that allow fewer (or other) freedoms. But the sparsely worded document is open to interpretation, and clauses of only a few words are often at the heart of national debates. The Bill of Rights was meant to protect individual liberties; but the needs of some individuals clash with those of society as a whole, and when this happens someone has to decide where to draw the line. Thus the Constitution becomes a battleground between the rights of individuals to do as they please and the responsibility of the government to protect its citizens. The First Amendment's guarantee of "freedom of speech," for example, leads to a number of difficult questions. Some forms of expression, such as burning an American flag, lead to public outrage—but nevertheless are said to be protected by the First Amendment. Other types of expression that most people find objectionable, such as sexually explicit material involving children, are not protected because they are considered harmful. The question is not only where to draw the line, but how to do this without infringing on the personal liberties on which the United States was built.

The Bill of Rights raises many other questions about individual rights and the societal "good." Is a prayer before a high school football game an "establishment of religion" prohibited by the First Amendment? Does the Second Amendment's promise of "the right to bear arms" include concealed handguns? Is stopping and frisking someone standing on a corner known to be frequented by drug dealers a form of "unreasonable search and seizure" in violation of the Fourth Amendment? Although the nine-member U.S. Supreme Court has the ultimate authority in interpreting the Constitution, its answers do not always satisfy the public. When a group of nine people—sometimes by a five-to-four vote—makes a decision that affects the lives of hundreds of millions, public outcry can be expected. And the composition of the Court does change over time, so even a landmark decision is not guaranteed to stand forever. The limits of constitutional protection are always in flux.

These issues make headlines, divide courts, and decide elections. They are the questions most worthy of national debate, and this series aims to cover them as thoroughly as possible. Each volume sets out some of the key arguments surrounding a particular issue, even some views that most people consider extreme or radical—but presents a balanced perspective on the issue. Excerpts from the relevant laws and judicial opinions and references to central concepts, source material, and advocacy groups help the reader to explore the issues even further and to read "the letter of the law" just as the legislatures and the courts have established it.

It may seem that some debates—such as those over capital punishment and abortion, debates with a strong moral component—will never be resolved. But American history offers numerous examples of controversies that once seemed insurmountable but now are effectively settled, even if only on the surface. Abolitionists met with widespread resistance to their efforts to end slavery, and the controversy over that issue threatened to cleave the nation in two; but today public debate over the merits of slavery would be unthinkable, though racial inequalities still plague the nation. Similarly unthinkable at one time was suffrage for women and minorities, but this is now a matter of course. Distributing information about contraception once was a crime. Societies change, and attitudes change, and new questions of social justice are raised constantly while the old ones fade into irrelevancy.

Whatever the root of the controversy, the books in POINT/ COUNTERPOINT seek to explain to the reader the origins of the debate, the current state of the law, and the arguments on both sides. The goal of the series is to inform the reader about the issues facing not only American politicians, but all of the nation's citizens, and to encourage the reader to become more actively involved in resolving these debates, as a voter, a concerned citizen, a journalist, an activist, or an elected official. Democracy is based on education, and every voice counts—so every opinion must be an informed one.

The long-simmering national debate over whether people have a right to die intensified in 2004–2005, as the nation watched the state of Florida, Congress, the President, and the U.S. Supreme intervene in Michael Schiavo's efforts to remove the feeding tube that was keeping his wife, Terri, alive. This volume examines some of the arguments made by those who supported Mr. Schiavo and by those who supported Ms. Schiavo's parents in their effort to keep their daughter alive. An important fundamental question is whether the states should try to protect the lives of people who are terminally ill and do not want to live or those who are unresponsive—in "persistent vegetative states"—and whose families do not wish to preserve them in such a state. Right-to-die supporters argue that the state should not intrude in such personal matters, while opponents counter that it is these most vulnerable people who most need the states' protection. Because the U.S. Supreme Court has ruled that states have a great deal of leeway in setting the standards for determining whether an unresponsive person would have wished to remain on life support, advocates on both sides of the debate have brought their arguments to the statehouses. While states take various approaches to sustaining life, voters in Oregon have enacted a controversial law that allows physicians to prescribe lethal doses of medication for the purpose of enabling terminally ill patients to commit suicide. The federal government unsuccessfully tried to disable Oregon's system, and the issue of physician-assisted suicide remains controversial in many of the other 49 states. This volume examines these controversies and the even more polarizing question of euthanasia, sometimes called "mercy killing."

History of the Euthanasia Debate

"Is he dead now?"

"He's dying now."

This chilling voice-over exchange between Mike Wallace and Dr. Jack Kevorkian was heard in homes across the United States as viewers watched grainy video footage. The scene showed Dr. Kevorkian injecting drugs into a bespectacled man in a plaid shirt, lying on a bed. The man's head rolled back and to the side.

"He's dead," the voice-over continued.

The date was November 22, 1998, and acclaimed news show *60 Minutes* was broadcasting a scene Dr. Kevorkian had filmed during one of his many self-described "mercy killings." The man on the bed was Thomas Youk, a 52-year-old who suffered from amyotrophic lateral sclerosis (ALS), commonly known as Lou Gehrig's disease. Mr. Youk had suffered from the disease for two years, to the point that he could not feed himself and often choked on his own saliva. In an effort to end his suffering, Mr. Youk had his family ask Dr. Kevorkian to assist him in his suicide. Dr. Kevorkian used this opportunity to garner attention for his crusade against laws prohibiting physician-assisted suicide. His plan worked. Following the *60 Minutes* show, the state of Michigan arrested Dr. Kevorkian for first-degree murder. He was tried, found guilty of second-degree murder, and sentenced to 10 to 25 years in state prison.[1]

The Kevorkian case highlights America's divide over questions involving the right to die. Although right-to-die issues have recently gained broader media attention from cases such as Kevorkian's and the Terri Schiavo case in 2005, the debate over how and when life should end is not new. Other persistent questions include who should make the crucial decisions involved and what level of governmental oversight should accompany the process.

Earliest History

Medical doctors often make critical ethical decisions when determining the best care for a patient. This ethical duty has long been rooted in the Hippocratic Oath, which physicians recite before they are allowed to work with patients. Modern medical ethics continue to rely on this 2,400-year-old oath because it emphasizes respect for human life and a physician's duty to protect that life. The classic oath includes the phrase, "I will neither give a deadly drug to anybody who asked for it, nor will I make a suggestion to this effect."[2] This early standard of medical ethics precluded any form of physician-assisted suicide or form of euthanasia.[3]

From the time that Hippocrates (ca. 460 B.C.–ca. 370 B.C.) wrote his oath through the mid-nineteenth century, right-to-die issues were seldom subject to public debate. As modern medicine remained in its infancy, most people died at home with family rather than under any medical care. Legislation in this area was

A History of Euthanasia

The controversy over euthanasia and physician-assisted suicide has existed for centuries. Ancient Greek and Roman philosophers spoke often and positively of suicide, calling it a "good death." Writings from that period include numerous accounts of people killing themselves through various means (poison, starvation, hanging, etc.), and the practice of asking a physician to assist them, both through prescription and administration, was common.

Acceptance of the idea of such a death was a part of Greek and Roman life until the rise of two formidable forces. One of these, the Christian faith, opposed suicide and viewed it as a grave sin. The Middle Ages saw a surge of Christianity, and debate over the subject halted because disapproval was adopted widely.

In the years leading up to the seventeenth century, suicide appeared as a topic for intellectual discussion. Discussion of suicide, physician-assisted suicide, and euthanasia appeared in multiple texts, including Thomas More's *Utopia*, John Bunyan's *Pilgrim's Progress,* and multiple plays by William Shakespeare. The sixteenth and seventeenth centuries proved to be an intellectual revolution concerning suicide and related topics, but the Christian principles governing such an act remained unchanged.

From 1715 to 1789, however, the debate once again appeared among intellectuals, and this time it gained wider consideration. Many leading thinkers of the time began to write about suicide, either justifying it or at least condemning punishment for the act. The acceptance of suicide, physician-assisted suicide, and euthanasia did not yet constitute the majority opinion, but this ideal still experienced a small but significant revival that allowed it to persist—with varying strength—for the next 300 years, until its resurgence in the twentieth century.

Disapproval of suicide was common at the beginning of the 1900s, both in Great Britain and the United States, but the laws of the two countries varied. Suicide had long been outlawed in Great Britain because taking one's own life was viewed as depriving the king of his "property" in the form of subjects, slaves, and revenue. Because the United States declared its independence from Great Britain and was no longer subject to the king, there seemed to be no legal reasoning to substantiate outlawing suicide. Suicide was still not a common practice; however, the thought that the act was not so immoral began to occur to the American people. For example, in 1906, legislators in both Ohio and Iowa drafted bills allowing voluntary euthanasia for people who met certain criteria. Neither bill passed, but they nonetheless represented a slow change in the way Americans were beginning to view end-of-life decisions.

From 1906 to World War II, support for euthanasia grew. In the United States, the Euthanasia Society of America was formed to lobby for the legalization of euthanasia. Although the acceptance of euthanasia, or "mercy killings" was rapidly increasing, the drama of World War II quickly changed the landscape.

After Nazi experiments in euthanasia, which resulted in the torture and mass genocide of the Jewish people and others—experiments that Hitler called "mercy killings"—were discovered, acceptance of euthanasia in the United States and elsewhere plummeted. Not only did Hitler succeed in murdering 6 million Jews, Gypsies, Poles, and others whose presence was considered "undesirable," but these mass murders also began with a secret order permitting doctors to put to death patients who suffered from physical or mental illnesses. The targeted patients included people with epilepsy and schizophrenia, as well as disabled infants. Nazi doctors killed 200,000 disabled men, women, and children by starvation, gassing, and other heinous methods. As expected, the news of such merciless "mercy killings" caused a severe backlash in American acceptance of euthanasia.

The association of euthanasia with Nazi Germany lasted for at least 20 years after World War II. Not until the late 1960s did advancements in medical technology compel an aging society to reconsider death from both biological and psychological points of view. Because of growing nuclear weaponry and the advancement of warfare technology, modern America became obsessed with death and dying, producing books, movies, magazines, radio broadcasts, and TV shows on the subject. This craze lasted through the 1970s, and the euthanasia debate received even more publicity when Karen Ann Quinlan's case was covered by the news media. Through the 1990s, public opinion and curiosity regarding euthanasia began to grow, and organizations in the United States experienced new acceptance among the public.

Court decisions such as *Cruzan*, *Schiavo*, and *Gonzales* began to shape public policy on euthanasia and physician-assisted suicide. With Oregon's passing of the Death With Dignity Act, public opinion about physician-assisted suicide began a rapid expansion. The same issues that plagued our ancestors still present difficult questions today: Is euthanasia ethical from a moral standpoint? A medical one? Should patients have the right to determine their own fate, or is it a physician's duty to do everything he or she can to try to prolong life? When is a life not worth living, and who should be able to decide such an answer? These questions and more guide the euthanasia debate.

Source: Ian Dowbiggin, *A Concise History of Euthanasia*. Oxford: Rowman & Littlefield, 2005, pp. 42–44.

sparse; the state of New York enacted the first legal prohibition against assisted suicide in 1828, when it outlawed both committing suicide and assisting someone to commit suicide.[4]

By the twentieth century, technological and medical advances extended life far beyond what had been possible only one or two generations earlier. With these advances in life-extending treatments came the necessity of going to hospitals for care. As people began spending their dying days in hospitals instead of their homes, questions were raised not only about the quantity of life, but also about the quality of life.[5]

These medical changes led members of the Ohio legislature to propose the first bill allowing assisted suicide in 1906. The bill did not pass, but it introduced the idea that the physician's role in the dying process might not be as simple as previously thought. An ethical debate also ensued; it would include religious and secular views on the value and importance of life, as well as society's duty to protect that life.[6]

In 1938, Reverend Charles Potter of New York established the Euthanasia Society of America (ESA), just three years after its London counterpart was founded. Despite its lack of success, Potter's ESA worked for decades to legalize medical assistance for euthanasia. The ESA was stymied by the global experience of World War II and the atrocities associated with Hitler's Final Solution. Nazi doctors provided a glaring example of how physicians could commit carnage in the name of science. Any suggestion of medical assistance in dying was frequently met with mental associations with concentration camps and genocide.[7]

By the 1960s, the ESA shifted its focus from euthanasia to individual choices made by patients. In 1967, the ESA and cooperating attorney Luis Kutner drafted the first "living will." This legally binding document allowed individuals to make their end-of-life wishes known before a crisis occurred. The introduction of the first modern euthanasia bill also occurred in 1967, in Florida. The Florida bill was defeated, but Idaho legislators attempted to pass a similar bill two years later; it met a similar fate.[8]

Modern Controversies

The modern right-to-die debate is framed in the public consciousness by four high-profile cases that span 30 years. These cases not only made the public more aware of these issues, they also provided legal clarification.

Quinlan

In 1976, the New Jersey Supreme Court heard arguments in a case that captured national attention. The court was asked to decide the fate of Karen Ann Quinlan, a 22-year-old patient who lay "debilitated and allegedly moribund" in the hospital after an incident at a party eight months earlier. The doctors treating her agreed that she could not survive without a respirator and was

> in a chronic and persistent vegetative state. No form of treatment which can cure or improve that condition is known or available. As nearly as may be determined, considering the guarded area of remote uncertainties characteristic of most medical science predictions, she can *never* be restored to cognitive or sapient life.[9]

In response to this diagnosis, Joseph Quinlan, Karen's father, asked that she be removed from the respirator and that no other extraordinary medical intervention take place. The hospital refused, and the court case that ensued eventually ended up before the New Jersey Supreme Court. Joseph Quinlan argued on behalf of both himself and his daughter that government interference with their right-to-die decision violated Constitutional protections to the free exercise of religion (First Amendment), was a cruel and unusual punishment (Eighth Amendment), and that it violated Karen's right to privacy (Fourth and Fourteenth amendments). The Court ruled in favor of Joseph Quinlan, agreeing that continued state intervention would violate Karen's privacy rights.[10] Based on the court's decision, Karen's respirator was removed. To the amazement of many, Karen continued to breathe on her own and remained alive, yet unimproved from her impaired state, for 10 more years. She died in 1985 from pneumonia.[11]

State legislatures across the country responded to the Quinlan controversy by passing right-to-die statutes. These statutes varied by state, but they all took into account the issues raised by the Quinlan case and the general common-law consensus that competent individuals had a right to refuse lifesaving treatment.[12] The problem that confronted many involved in these issues centered on the fact that the case had only gone as far as the state supreme court; the U.S. Supreme Court never explicitly ruled on this issue. Fifteen years later, the Supreme Court did just that.

Cruzan

In 1990, America's attention was once again riveted to questions involving the right to die. In January 1983, state troopers found Nancy Cruzan next to a Missouri roadway after her car had crashed and flipped over. When paramedics arrived, their examinations determined that Nancy had been without oxygen for 14 to 16 minutes. Doctors ascertained that Nancy was severely brain damaged and inserted a feeding tube to keep her nourished and hydrated.

She was readmitted to the hospital in October 1983, when it was determined that rehabilitative therapy would not help. Nancy's parents asked the hospital staff to remove the feeding tube. The staff refused, claiming that, according to Missouri law, they could only stop feeding if they were provided with a court order. The Cruzans filed a petition to have the court order the removal of the feeding tube, and the trial judge agreed. Yet, the state of Missouri and Nancy's *guardian ad litem* appealed. (A *guardian ad litem* is a third party appointed by the court to protect the interests of a minor or incapacitated person when they cannot speak appropriately for their own interests.) The state supreme court sided with the state and found that the Cruzans had not provided clear and convincing evidence that their daughter would wish to have the feedings stop if she were able to speak for herself.[13]

In December 1989, the United States Supreme Court heard the case of *Cruzan v. Director, Missouri Department of Health*. The Court's findings changed the face of right-to-die cases. In a 5 to 4 majority opinion, Chief Justice William Rehnquist explained that there was no Constitutional right for an incompetent patient to remove lifesaving measures. By reviewing previous cases, Chief Justice Rehnquist examined the legal history of the right to die. He found that previous cases were based on two concerns. The first involved the patient's fundamental right to privacy. The Supreme Court has repeatedly ruled that intimate decisions are private, and that the state should interfere in how people make those decisions only if the state has an incredibly important interest. If patients were not allowed to refuse treatment, then their fundamental right to privacy would be infringed. The second basis for earlier decisions used the common-law rule of informed consent. Informed consent is the legal rule that requires doctors to get a patient's permission before performing any sort of treatment on the person. Before getting this permission, the doctor must also make clear to the patient what is involved in the medical action (risks, side effects, etc.) Without this permission, doctors are not supposed to treat patients. Ultimately, the majority found that the right-to-privacy argument was not as strong as the common-law rule of informed consent. Therefore, the issue was a matter for states to decide, not the federal courts.[14]

This meant that states had the authority to regulate what criteria must be met in order to remove lifesaving measures for incompetent persons. In the case of Missouri, this meant that the guardian of an incompetent person must demonstrate through "clear and convincing evidence" that the person would not want to continue life in a permanent vegetative state.[15] In legal terms, "clear and convincing evidence" is "evidence indicating that the thing to be proved is highly probably or reasonably certain."[16] This middle standard for evidence falls between the standards used in civil trials ("preponderance of the evidence") and those used in criminal trials ("beyond a reasonable doubt").[17]

Although the Court ruled against the Cruzans, the ruling was groundbreaking in that, for the first time, the Supreme Court recognized a competent person's right to reject lifesaving treatment. As Chief Justice Rehnquist stated,

> [T]he principle that a competent person has a constitutionally protected liberty interest in refusing unwanted medical treatment may be inferred from our prior decisions . . . [and] for purposes of this case, we assume that the United States Constitution would grant a competent person a constitutionally protected right to refuse lifesaving hydration and nutrition.[18]

The Court went on to state that this desire to reject treatment could be inferred from pre-incompetent statements made by an individual.[19]

Youk and Kevorkian

The third controversy that raised awareness of this debate centers on the case of Dr. Jack Kevorkian. As stated earlier, on September 17, 1998, Dr. Kevorkian injected Thomas Youk, a 52-year-old ALS sufferer, with a cocktail of drugs These drugs sedated Mr. Youk, then caused his breathing to slow and his heart to stop. Michigan's law against physician-assisted suicide had gone into effect just three weeks earlier.[20]

By his own admission, Dr. Kevorkian had participated in almost 130 deaths. He had been tried in the courts four times before 1998, for assisting suicides. Each trial ended in either a mistrial or an acquittal. The Youk situation was different for two reasons: (1) A videotape of the procedure was available. (2) Previous deaths had all involved suicide, with the ill person taking his or her own life through overdose, or through the use of Dr. Kevorkian's *Thanatron* (Greek for "death machine"). Dr. Kevorkian's involvement with Youk, however, included Kevorkian himself injecting the drug, thus changing the situation from a suicide to an act of euthanasia or "mercy killing."[21]

Melody Youk (left), widow of Thomas Youk, meets with Dr. Jack Kevorkian during the trial in which Kevorkian was charged with the murder of Thomas Youk. Kevorkian had videotaped Youk's assisted suicide and allowed it to broadcast on *60 Minutes*, after which Kevorkian was charged with the murder.

When the police arrested Kevorkian this time, they charged him with first-degree murder. The jury heard the case and returned a guilty verdict. In response, Judge Jessica Cooper sentenced Kevorkian to 10 to 25 years in state prison. After serving 8 years of the term, Kevorkian is scheduled to be released on parole in June 2007 because of health concerns. As a condition of his release, Kevorkian has promised to refrain from assisting in any more deaths.[22]

Schiavo

On February 25, 1990, emergency crews rushed Terri Schiavo, a 26-year-old resident of Pinnelas Park, Florida, to the hospital after she collapsed in her home. Doctors later determined that a potassium imbalance caused by an eating disorder disrupted oxygen supplies to her brain for almost five minutes. This disruption

Important Terms in the Right-to-die Debate

Brain dead: "We have an internal vegetative regulation which controls body temperature which controls breathing, which controls to a considerable degree blood pressure, which controls to some degree heart rate, which controls chewing, swallowing and which controls sleeping and waking. We have a more highly developed brain which is uniquely human which controls our relation to the outside world, our capacity to talk, to see, to feel, to sing, to think. Brain death necessarily must mean the death of both of these functions of the brain, vegetative and the sapient. Therefore, the presence of any function which is regulated or governed or controlled by the deeper parts of the brain which in laymen's terms might be considered purely vegetative would mean that the brain is not biologically dead."*

Euthanasia: "The act or practice of killing or bringing about the death of a person who suffers from an incurable disease or condition, especially a painful one, for reasons of mercy. Euthanasia is sometimes regarded by the law as second-degree murder, manslaughter, or criminally negligent homicide.

Active euthanasia: Euthanasia performed by a facilitator (usually a physician) who not only provides the means of death but also carries out the final death-causing act.

Involuntary euthanasia: Euthanasia of a competent, nonconsenting person.

Nonvoluntary euthanasia: Euthanasia of an incompetent, and therefore nonconsenting, person.

Passive euthanasia: The act of allowing a terminally ill person to die by either withholding or withdrawing life-sustaining support such as a respirator or feeding tube.

caused permanent and severe neurological impairment requiring physicians to use a ventilator and feeding tube to keep Ms. Schiavo alive. Although the ventilator was later removed, the feeding tube remained, and doctors determined that Ms. Schiavo was in a persistent vegetative state, from which she was unlikely ever to recover. Her husband, Michael, was appointed her guardian.

Voluntary euthanasia: Euthanasia performed with the terminally ill person's consent.

Right to die: The right of a terminally ill person to refuse life-sustaining treatment.

Assisted suicide: The intentional act of providing a person with the medical means or the medical knowledge to commit suicide." **

Palliative care: "Palliative care is an approach that improves the quality of life of patients and their families facing the problem associated with life-threatening illness, through the prevention and relief of suffering by means of early identification and impeccable assessment and treatment of pain and other problems, physical, psychosocial, and spiritual."***

Persistent vegetative state: "Vegetative state describes a body which is functioning entirely in terms of its internal controls. It maintains temperature. It maintains heart beat and pulmonary ventilation. It maintains digestive activity. It maintains reflex activity of muscles and nerves for low level conditioned responses. But there is no behavioral evidence of either self-awareness or awareness of the surroundings in a learned manner."†

*In re Quinlan, 70 N.J. 10 (1976): 25. Testimony of Dr. Fred Plum.
**Bryan A. Garner, ed. Black's Law Dictionary, 7th ed. St. Paul, Minn.: West Group, 1999.
***"Palliative Care." World Health Organization's Web page. Available online. URL: http://www.who.int/hiv/topics/palliative/care/en/.
†In re Jobes, 108 N.J. 394 (1987): 438. Testimony of Dr. Fred Plum.

After Michael had a falling out with Ms. Schiavo's parents, Robert and Mary Shindler, a legal battle erupted over Terri's care. This battle intensified when, in 1998, Michael petitioned the court to have Terri's feeding tube removed. According to Florida state law, termination of life-sustaining medical procedures for incompetent patients requires "clear and convincing evidence" that, if the patient were competent to decide or communicate for him- or herself, he or she would want the measures terminated.[23]

The events that followed brought this family tragedy, which had originated in Florida, to the halls of Congress, the president of the United States, and the U.S. Supreme Court. Before the controversy was over, the U.S. House of Representatives and Senate passed a bill that moved jurisdiction of this case to the federal courts for review, which President George W. Bush promptly signed.[24]

From 2000 to 2005, Terri Schiavo's feeding tube was removed and reinserted twice more before it was removed for the final time on March 18, 2005. (She died 13 days later).[25] Her case was heard at every level of the judicial branch of government, and politicians on both sides of the right-to-die debate took strong stands behind the participants in this controversy. Because of this, the relevance of Schiavo's case is not in any groundbreaking legal precedent, but rather in the political uproar it caused. News channels covered the drama through every step of the process through 2005. The Schiavo case validated the recurring theme in right-to-die cases—sincere people on both sides of the issue continue to have strong feelings about end-of-life decisions and who is entitled to make those decisions.

The Controversy Today

As history shows, controversy over the "right to die" includes several issues. These include the correct level of life prolonging medical intervention, the ethics of actively taking one's own life, and the ethics of taking the life of another person. Yet, when most people discuss the right to die, they are typically talking about assisted suicide and euthanasia. *Assisted suicide* is defined as "[t]he intentional act of providing someone with the medical means or medical knowledge to commit suicide," whereas most definitions of *euthanasia* call it "[t]he act or practice of killing or bringing about the death of a person who suffers from an incurable disease or condition, esp[ecially] a painful one, for reasons of mercy."[26]

The distinction between suicide, or the taking of one's own life, and euthanasia, participating in the death of another, is an important part of the controversy. Although some argue that these distinctions are academic and not relevant to the realities of end-of-life decisions, for others, these distinctions are highly important. One place where such distinctions become important is in legal statutes, where this difference is closely monitored.[27] As later chapters will examine, the newest, and arguably most controversial, element of this debate is Oregon's Death With Dignity Act, a law that allows physicians in Oregon to prescribe lethal drugs to patients, if the patient willingly participates in the multiple steps required in the process.[28]

Summary

Civilization has dealt with right-to-die issues from the earliest times. Modern debate over the right to die has intensified in the United States, especially with high-profile cases. Starting in the 1960s with the *Quinlan* case, lower courts have recognized an individual's right to refuse treatment. In the 1980s, the U.S. Supreme Court examined the *Cruzan* case and found that, under the U.S. Constitution, people have the right to refuse treatment, even if death results. The Court also ruled that, although people have this right to personal liberty, the states have a right to have standards in place on how that right may be exercised, particularly if a guardian is involved.

In the mid 1990s, Dr. Jack Kevorkian gained international attention when he participated in an act of voluntary euthanasia, which he taped and later showed on a national news show. This high-profile action led to Dr. Kevorkian's arrest and confinement. Finally, in 2004, Americans were riveted to the news networks as they watched the drama unfold over the Terri Schiavo case, which, for the first time, involved politicians inserting themselves directly into a specific right-to-die controversy. Although the last two controversies did not break new legal ground, they did bring a heightened sensitivity to the issue among the broader public. These controversies also highlight the various issues found under the umbrella of "right to die," including the distinctions between suicide and euthanasia.

States Have a Duty to Protect Life in All Forms

Citizens entrust their government with incredible power. In the United States, this trust relies on the belief that the government will use that power to strike a proper balance between ensuring order and protecting an individual's freedom. Many people believe that this balance between order and freedom is best achieved when the government protects its citizens' lives in all forms. They rest their belief that the government has a duty to protect life in the idea that all life is sacred and valuable, that protecting life will create the most effective order, and that it is unjust to allow one life to be valued differently from another.

Life is sacred and invaluable.

Arguments over the right to die ultimately rest on the value placed on human life. Cultures and societies around the world have struggled with how human life should be valued and protected. In ancient societies, life was valued and protected based on social status, such as one's connections to royalty or one's position in religious hierarchies. One's position in life determined whether or not that life was worth saving.

In the modern world, most people recognize the intrinsic value of human life. Many governments rest on the ideal of protecting human life. In the United States, the country's founding documents recognize the importance of protecting life. The Declaration of Independence states,

> We hold these truths to be self-evident, that all men are created equal, that they are endowed by their Creator with certain unalienable Rights, that among these are Life, Liberty and the pursuit of Happiness. That to secure these rights, Governments are instituted among Men, deriving their just powers from the consent of the governed.[29]

According to the Declaration of Independence, and the U.S. Constitution that followed it, the purpose of the government is to protect people's rights. The right to life rests high in the order of rights that the government must protect. These documents specify that all people have a right to life that the government must protect, regardless of the individuals' status in society.

The philosophical foundation for this approach goes back to the early Greek philosophers, such as Plato and Aristotle. They discouraged suicide and encouraged people to live the life that nature intended for them. In book nine of Plato's *Law*, he argued, "Suicide . . . deprives [a man] by violence of his appointed share of life, not because the law of the state requires him, . . . but who from sloth or want of manliness imposes upon himself an unjust penalty."[30] Aristotle went further, arguing that suicide was always wrong because it deprived society of a member.[31]

Later, the English philosopher Thomas Hobbes wrote in his treatise *Leviathan* that people without civil government live in a state of nature where life is "solitary, poore [*sic*], nasty, brutish, and short." The only way to protect life and make it more fulfilling is to bind together under a system of government. In order for life to be protected under this system of government, order must be created. The foundation of all order is the security of each person in knowing that his or her life will be protected. The very reason people create civil societies is to protect and improve their lives.[32]

Most people do not argue that life should be protected based on philosophical arguments, however. More often, religious beliefs inform people's arguments that life should be protected. Christians have a long history of speaking out on the "sanctity of human life." In the early church, Saint Augustine of Hippo wrote extensively on suicide, noting that it was forbidden in all cases except one—if God directly commanded it. Even in situations of great suffering, a person is to accept the suffering as a part of life that God allows.

Thomas Aquinas later built on this idea when he argued that suicide is a moral wrong because it disrupts the natural order, harms one's community, and is a sin against God. This last argument was most important to Aquinas, for he argued that taking one's life is stealing from God (who owns all life and determines who lives and who dies). This sin is compounded because

John Stemberger on the Right to Die

There is no "right to die" under the constitution or under any moral claim. Life is a gift given by God and should only be taken by God or his naturally ordained process of death. As obvious as it may seem, one needs to look no further than the ten commandments for the timeless and controlling moral principle to guide the outcome of this case: "Thou shall not kill."

Source: John Stemberger, *The Terri Schiavo Controversy—Facts, Myths and Christian Perspectives.* Available online. URL: http://www.frc.org/get.cfm?i=LH05C02.

suicide is so final; it is a sin for which a person cannot later ask forgiveness. That is why, for many centuries, the Catholic Church relied on Aquinas's arguments and would not allow those who committed suicide to be buried in Catholic cemeteries.[33]

In 1980, the Vatican reaffirmed centuries of teaching against suicide and murder in its Declaration on Euthanasia, which begins,

> In this regard, the Second Vatican Ecumenical Council solemnly reaffirmed the lofty dignity of the human person, and in a special way his or her right to life. The Council therefore condemned crimes against life "such as any type of murder, genocide, abortion, euthanasia, or willful suicide." Intentionally causing one's own death, or suicide, is therefore equally as wrong as murder; such an action on the part of a person is to be considered as a rejection of God's sovereignty and loving plan."[34]

Protestants are equally troubled by issues of suicide and euthanasia. Based on the belief that all people are made in God's image, and that life is given to people by God with the purpose

Jewish Views of Euthanasia and Suicide

Jews do not interpret the fifth commandment, "Thou shalt not kill," as referring to suicide. However, in Judaism, the preservation of human life is valued above almost all else. In Jewish law, nearly every other consideration is put second to saving a life. Both fasting and circumcision, for example, are to be postponed if the practice might endanger the individual's health. The premature ending of a person's life is completely counter to this Jewish perspective, so suicide and euthanasia are unequivocally rejected in modern Judaism.

Source: "Euthanasia and Judaism: Jewish Views of Euthanasia and Suicide." *Euthanasia.* Available online. URL: http://www.religionfacts.com/euthanasia/judaism.htm.

of service to others, many Protestants share the Catholic belief that shortening the natural expanse of one's life is a sin. The largest Protestant denomination in the United States, the Southern Baptist Convention, resolved in 2001:

> That the messengers to the Southern Baptist Convention meeting in New Orleans, Louisiana, June 12 to 13, 2001, affirm our belief that every human life, including the life of the terminally ill, disabled, or clinically depressed patient, is sacred and ought to be protected against unnecessary harm; and be it further resolved, that we find legalized euthanasia immoral ethically, unnecessary medically, and unconscionable socially.[35]

Judaism also tends to argue against suicide and euthanasia. Stephen Resnicoff of DePaul University College of Law explains that Jewish law recognizes both the importance of preserving human life and the ownership of that life by God. Therefore, ending a life, either through suicide or assisting suicide, is prohibited. Many Jewish theologians find a basis for this restriction in the Talmud's exposition on the story of Adam,

> [O]nly a single human being was created in the world [at first] to teach that if any person has caused a single soul to perish, Scripture regards him as if he had caused an entire world to perish; and if any human being saves a single soul, Scripture regards him as if he had saved an entire world.[36]

Other religious groups also place prohibitions on prematurely ending life. Muslims abide by the Quran, which explicitly states, "You shall not kill yourselves. GOD is merciful towards you[,]" and, "You shall not kill any person—for GOD has made life sacred—except in the course of justice."[37] Most Buddhists oppose involuntary and voluntary euthanasia, or any form of suicide that would lead to a disturbance of the reincarnation cycle.[38] In both secular and religious rationales for protecting human life, all lives are sacred and valuable and should be saved and protected.

The basic duty of government is to create order.

As Thomas Hobbes stated in *Leviathan*, the fundamental purpose of society is to create order. In the United States, the Constitution requires the government to balance that order with protection of the individual's rights. The most fundamental of all human rights is the right to life. Many people who argue against the right to die claim that the right to life is intrinsic to

John Paul II on Life-sustaining Treatments and Vegetative State

The sick person in a vegetative state, awaiting recovery or a natural end, still has the right to basic health care (nutrition, hydration, cleanliness, warmth, etc.), and to the prevention of complications related to his confinement to bed. He also has the right to appropriate rehabilitative care and to be monitored for clinical signs of eventual recovery.

I should like particularly to underline how the administration of water and food, even when provided by artificial means, always represents a *natural means* of preserving life, not a *medical act*. Its use, furthermore, should be considered, in principle, *ordinary* and *proportionate*, and as such morally obligatory, insofar as and until it is seen to have attained its proper finality, which in the present case consists in providing nourishment to the patient and alleviation of his suffering ...

In this regard, I recall what I wrote in the Encyclical *Evangelium Vitae*, making it clear that "by *euthanasia in the true and proper sense* must be understood an action or omission which by its very nature and intention brings about death, with the purpose of eliminating all pain"; such an act is always "a serious violation of the law of God, since it is the deliberate and morally unacceptable killing of a human person."

Source: Address of John Paul II to the Participants in the International Congress on "Life-Sustaining Treatments and Vegetative State: Scientific Advances and Ethical Dilemmas," March 20, 2004

a person and cannot be waived. Opponents argue that waiving the right to life is similar to the right to sell oneself into slavery: it is a claim that invalidates itself.[39]

These opponents point out that the government is misdirected when it allows death instead of promoting life. As detailed in the New York State's Department of Health Task Force Report on Life and the Law, some people oppose physician-assisted suicide and other forms of euthanasia because of the disproportionate impact it may have on society:

> As expressed by one doctor who manages a Latino health clinic, legalizing assisted suicide would pose special dangers for members of minority populations whose primary concern is access to needed care, not assistance to die more quickly. "In the abstract, it sounds like a wonderful idea, but in a practical sense it would be a disaster. My concern is for Latinos and other minority groups that might get disproportionately counseled to opt for physician-assisted suicide."[40]

Because one of the government's duties is to avoid disproportionate impact of laws on citizens, allowing euthanasia may lead to perversions in the system.

There is no way to decide which lives are worth living, so all lives should be protected.

Who will determine who lives and who dies is one of the most troubling aspects of the right-to-die debate. This is because whoever makes the decisions determines which lives are worth living and which are not. The importance of these decisions is heightened by the irreversible nature of the result.

In what many right-to-die proponents see as the easiest situation, people would make their own decisions about ending their lives. The difficulty with this approach is that many people who claim they want to end their lives based on some terminal or incurable infirmity are typically also dealing with

depression or other psychological problems that impair their ability to make informed decisions. This concern over undiagnosed depression as a motivation for suicide has led many medical organizations to draft ethics guidelines to prohibit physician-assisted suicide.[41]

The Pew Research Center's poll data on right-to-die attitudes, although not conclusive, shows that whereas many people favor allowing others the right to die, most people would not terminate their own treatment. Even those faced with hypothetical pain and suffering indicated that they would still want the doctors to do all they could to save them.[42] This kind of statistical data cannot reliably indicate an individual's decision, but it does show the attitudes of people who are not currently hampered by depression or other mental infirmity associated with end-of-life suffering toward these issues.

The other concern is that a guardian will not appropriately represent the wishes of the incapacitated patient. As the Supreme Court pointed out in the *Cruzan* case,

> Not all incompetent patients will have loved ones available to serve as surrogate decision makers. And even where family members are present, there will, of course, be some unfortunate situations in which family members will not act to

The Islamic Code of Medical Ethics

Mercy killing, like suicide, finds no support except in the atheistic way of thinking that believes that our life on this earth is followed by void. The claim of killing for painful hopeless illness is also refuted, for there is no human pain that cannot be largely conquered by medication or by suitable neurosurgery.

Source: *The Islamic Code of Medical Ethics, endorsed by the First International Conference on Islamic Medicine.* Kuwait: Islamic Organization of Medical Sciences, 1981, p. 6

protect a patient. A State is entitled to guard against potential abuses in such situations.[43] (internal quotes omitted)

If a surrogate makes the decision, he or she may not represent the wishes of the patient. This potential lack of appropriate representation limits the patient's autonomy, thus invalidating any argument concerning the right of the incapacitated patient.

———●———————●———————●———

Summary

Based on both philosophical ideas and religious beliefs, human life is sacred and should be protected whenever possible. The U.S. Constitution and other founding documents recognize an inalienable right to life that the government has a duty to protect. Theologians also believe that life is sacred as a gift given by a Supreme Being, and therefore it is a violation of religious law to harm this gift of life. Since life is sacred and valuable, the government has a duty to protect it, as part of government's job in creating order. There is also no way to distinguish which lives are worth living and which are not, and it is unethical to try to do so. Therefore, the government must protect all lives to the best of its ability.

End-of-life Decisions Are Personal Matters

Throughout American history, citizens have fought for freedom. From the Founding Fathers' fight for political freedom from a distant monarch, to the abolitionist movement for the freedom of individuals from slavery, to civil rights workers, who still fight for freedom from social and legal discrimination, America has been a nation intent on protecting the freedom of the individual. Today, America is faced with yet another fight for freedom: the freedom to make choices about the end of life.

Forcing citizens to suffer from incurable diseases as they waste away is cruel, and for those advocating such forced life-prolonging measures, certain realities are being ignored. End-of-life decisions are personal matters that should not involve government interference for three reasons: (1) End-of-life matters typically fall within the realm of personal freedom, in which the U.S. Constitution prohibits the government's interference. (2) End-of-life decisions are private medical matters that should be protected as private. (3) Prolonging a patient's life against his or her wishes wastes resources that the patient may not want to drain from his or her family or society.

Personal freedom and autonomy are paramount.

People who claim to be protecting life often argue that life is sacred and should not be ended artificially. They claim that the state has no higher duty than to protect the lives of all its citizens. Yet these claims fail to recognize that life is already measured, and society often ends lives prematurely. The clearest example would be the death penalty, which is still legal in many states in the United States. It is argued that those who receive the death penalty do not want to die but receive death as a punishment, whereas those who seek death are denied it, even though they have broken no laws.

In other instances, the nation has applauded those who willingly give their lives for their country. Military personnel are awarded posthumous medals for acts of valor, such as jumping on a grenade or taking a bullet for a comrade. The heroes of the military, fire department, police department, and other groups who keep people safe at great personal risk to their lives are lauded, not accused of cheapening life.

Protecting one life at the expense of another is not the only reason that Americans have allowed life to end. Going back to this country's Founding Fathers, Patrick Henry's historic speech of 1775 ends with the oft quoted, "[I]s life so dear, or peace so sweet, as to be purchased at the price of chains and slavery? Forbid it, Almighty God! I know not what course others may take; but as for me, give me liberty or give me death!"[44] Clearly, certain principles are worth dying for. As a nation, America does not protect all life, nor does it even promote protecting life at the expense of all else, so the question becomes, How does society determine who lives and who dies?

Karen Ann Quinlan, shown above in an undated photograph, fell into a coma when she was 21. After Quinlan went
several months with no improvement, her parents asked
to have her removed from life support, but the hospital
refused, setting the stage for a controversial court case.

Valuing life, and determining what is more important than living, are decisions typically left to the individual. Those who give their lives for others or for ideals are revered because they chose to make that sacrifice. Their actions would not be as laudable if they were forced to kill themselves. It is the central idea of personal autonomy that makes the difference. The United States was founded on this ideal of personal liberty and autonomy.

Those who have incurable diseases with nothing in their futures except pain and suffering may wish to end their lives. This could be because they do not want to endure the pain, but in some instances ending the suffering is an act of compassion toward friends and family. By ending the pain, the patient makes the decision to limit the suffering of those close to him or her. In this way, the family does not have to bear the financial burden of extended medical treatments that do little but prolong suffering, nor do they have to bear the emotional trauma of watching a loved one waste away.

In the end, only the individual truly knows how much pain and suffering he or she experiences. Even the Supreme Court recognizes that no one should be required to endure unnecessary medical procedures if he or she wishes to allow nature to take its course.[45] Although the Fourteenth Amendment to the U.S. Constitution states, "nor shall any state deprive any person of life, liberty or property, without due process of law," it does not grant the government the power to extend that life if the person does not want to continue to live.[46] Likewise, if a person does not wish to continue his life, then the government should not make him do so. The Fourteenth Amendment gives states the power to protect the lives of people through the use of police power. It does not give the state the right to force people to continue their lives. A person does not have to use his right to life any more than a person must use his right to free speech. The state's job is to make sure the person has the opportunity to exercise his rights. It does not have the right to force people to do the same.

Medical privacy should be protected.

Constitutional interpretations involving a right to privacy are also involved in debates over the right to life. As Mr. Quinlan argued to the New Jersey Supreme Court in his lawsuit to remove his daughter from a respirator, medical decisions are private matters.[47] Mr. Quinlan is not alone in his desire to have medical information and decisions kept private. A 2004 Harris Interactive Poll found that 78 percent of respondents felt it important that their medical information be kept private.[48]

FROM THE BENCH

In Re Quinlan, 70 N.J. 10 (1976)

On an April night in 1975, Karen Ann Quinlan was out with her friends when she suddenly stopped breathing. After two 15-minute periods of no oxygen to her brain and multiple attempts at cardiopulmonary resuscitation (CPR), she was rushed to the hospital. With a high fever, unresponsive pupils, a lack of response to pain, and an inability to breathe on her own, she was soon diagnosed as being in a chronic, persistent vegetative state and was put on a respirator. Acting as her guardian, her father, Joseph Quinlan, asked that her respirator be removed in order to allow Karen to die naturally rather than prolong a life with no hope of rehabilitation. Excerpts from the opinion of the court, which decided in favor of Joseph Quinlan, are cited below.

> Dr. Korein['s testimony] also told of the unwritten and unspoken standard of medical practice implied in the foreboding initials DNR (do not resuscitate), as applied to the extraordinary terminal case:
>
>> Cancer, metastatic cancer, involving the lungs, the liver, the brain, multiple involvements, the physician may or may not write: Do not resuscitate. [I]t could be said to the nurse: if this man stops breathing don't resuscitate him. No physician that I know personally is going to try and resuscitate a man riddled with cancer and in agony and he stops breathing. They are not going to put him on a respirator. I think that would be the height of misuse of technology.
>
> We have no hesitancy in deciding, in the instant diametrically opposite case, that no external compelling interest of the State could compel Karen to

This finding reflects the long tradition of medical privacy in the United States, originating in the common-law created doctor-patient privilege.

The United States Supreme Court agrees that privacy is an important right that must be protected. In a string of cases, the Court found that the government had no business looking into or interfering with private decisions. In the case of *Griswold v. Connecticut*, the Supreme Court found that people have a privacy interest in their medical decisions related to birth control.[49]

---

endure the unendurable, only to vegetate a few measurable months with no realistic possibility of returning to any semblance of cognitive or sapient life. We perceive no thread of logic distinguishing between such a choice on Karen's part and a similar choice which, under the evidence in this case, could be made by a competent patient terminally ill, riddled by cancer and suffering great pain; such a patient would not be resuscitated or put on a respirator in the example described by Dr. Korein, and a fortiori would not be kept against his will on a respirator ...

Ultimately there comes a point at which the individual's rights overcome the State interest. It is for that reason that we believe Karen's choice, if she were competent to make it, would be vindicated by the law. Her prognosis is extremely poor,—she will never resume cognitive life. And the bodily invasion is very great,—she requires 24 hour intensive nursing care, antibiotics, the assistance of a respirator, a catheter and feeding tube.... Doctors, [in order to] to treat a patient, must deal with medical tradition and past case histories. They must be guided by what they know. The extent of their training, their experience, consultation with other physicians, must guide their decision-making processes in providing care to their patient. The nature, extent and duration of care by societal standards is the responsibility of a physician. The morality and conscience of our society places this responsibility in the hands of the physician. What justification is there to remove it from the control of the medical profession and place it in the hands of the courts?

Source: *In Re Quinlan*, 70 N.J.10 (1976). Majority opinion by Chief Justice Hughes.

Later, in *Roe v. Wade,* the Court found a privacy right in ending a pregnancy.[50] Further, in 2003, the Court found in *Lawrence v. Texas* that consensual homosexual sex was a private matter in which the state should not interfere.[51] These privacy cases indicate a desire by the Court to interpret the Constitution in a way that protects individuals' privacy in the most intimate of matters. If the Court is willing to protect privacy in these instances, then it follows that they should protect privacy in the most intimate and private acts involved in end-of-life decision making.

Congress has also recognized the need for medical privacy, passing the Health Insurance Portability and Accountability Act, or HIPAA, in 1996. Among other issues involving health insurance, this law required medical providers to protect the privacy of patients.[52] Such measures indicate government officials' awareness that medical decisions are of the utmost importance, and their sensitive nature leads to a need for protecting their privacy.

Prolonging life against the patient's wishes wastes resources.

Beyond the liberty interests in being able to make one's own decisions about how one dies, there are also economic interests. Patients who are in a permanent vegetative state must be cared for around the clock. Others who have terminal diseases and wish to end their lives early to avoid the pain and loss of dignity will also need to be supported and maintained by either accumulated life assets or through the generosity of others.

For those who find this line of reasoning too strident and possibly amoral, the reality is that these kinds of decisions are already made on a daily basis. Not everyone gets all the treatments they want, either because they are not available in the patient's location, or the person cannot afford the treatment. Would it not be more moral to allow those who do not want to continue their suffering to end the pain, and use the available resources to help those who do want the treatments?

Nor is this argument strictly one of social utilitarianism. Clearly it would be wrong for society to find someone no longer useful and require them to commit suicide. But for some people who know they are dying and that there is little hope of a cure, they may wish not to use up all their assets on maintaining their decline. They may instead wish to pass those assets on to their children, other loved ones, or a charity.

Summary

Human life is sacred and invaluable, but if liberty and autonomy are stripped from individuals, then their lives are no longer sacrosanct. This is why, throughout U.S. history, personal liberty has been a right that is worth sacrificing one's life. The Founding Fathers recognized this ideal, which superseded even life, as Patrick Henry expressed when he stated, "Give me liberty or give me death." Because liberty is so important in the American system, the government should protect individual autonomy. One area where liberty is of high importance in relation to the right to die is in medical privacy. Both Congress and the Supreme Court recognize the importance of privacy in intimate issues. Through laws and judicial decisions, the branches of government support, and should continue to support, this important individual right to privacy. Finally, a person should have the right to determine how his or her assets should be passed on and not be required to use them to sustain life.

Without Clear Evidence of Intent, Life Support Should Be Administered

On Valentine's Day, 1993, an odd scene played out in a nursing home in Largo, Florida. Though details vary, all agree that Michael Schiavo and his father-in-law Bob Schindler had a bitter exchange of words over the money awarded from a malpractice case involving Terri Schiavo. While her husband and father fought over the money, Terri sat between them, strapped into a medical lounge chair. The split this argument caused ultimately led to a national event 11 years later, as Americans across the country watched the family controversy play out on national television. Throughout the fight, both in the room and later on the national stage, Terri Schiavo sat at the center of a dispute into which she no longer had any input. Although her wishes were ultimately the goal of the controversy, everyone but Terri participated in her fate.[53]

These kinds of family issues are not uncommon, and they only rarely get the media attention Terri Schiavo did in 2004.

The reality of these controversies, however, causes states across the nation to insert guidelines into their legal codes that provide guidance on how best to determine the wishes of those who cannot speak for themselves.

State-imposed standards are necessary.

Whether or not one agrees that individuals have a right to die, clearly any rule must have standards to protect those who cannot protect themselves. All legal questions involve objective standards so that laws can be applied justly, even when controversies are brought forward in different courts, possibly in different parts of the country. The greater the risk of injury, or the likelihood that an action is irreversible, the greater the protections and due process imposed by the legal system.

Because right-to-die cases involve the possibility of death—the ultimate irreversible condition—the greatest protections and standards are necessary. Myriad legal standards exist in right-to-die cases because there are so many aspects of these cases to consider. Who decides what is best for the incapacitated patient? If there is no advance directive, who best knows the wishes of the unconscious person? How can abuses be avoided? Will the hospital and doctors be protected from a lawsuit if they take someone off life support? What if they leave them on life support? When is someone "legally dead"? These and many other questions must be decided in every right-to-die case.

The importance of clear standards in questions of who gets to make decisions for the unconscious can be seen in a controversy that arose in 1987. Seventeen-year-old Phillip Rader suffered complications from surgery that left him with no brain activity, but through the use of machines and medicine, his heart was still beating and he was still breathing. The hospital wanted to shut down the machines, but the family refused. During the legal battle that ensued, problems arose over whether Phillip was dead. First, his birthday arrived before the court date for the Missouri Supreme Court hearing (scheduled for the same day as

Nancy Cruzan, in an undated photograph, was thrown from her car in an accident at age 25. She suffered severe brain damage and was declared to be in a persistent vegetative state. Her family fought for three years to have her feeding tube removed, eventually taking the case to the Supreme Court.

the Nancy Cruzan case.) Once 18, Phillip was legally considered emancipated, and his parents would no longer be his guardians. No clear standards existed as to whether his aging stopped at the moment of brain death, or if he was even alive.[54]

In a far more bizarre twist, questions over whether Phillip was alive led to a criminal conundrum. A psychiatric patient from another ward made his or her way into Phillip's room and removed his feeding tube and respirator. The damage done to the body during the removal contributed to Phillip's eventual death two weeks later. When Phillip's parents asked the police to do something, they were told that they could not arrest the psychiatric patient because, under the criminal law, Phillip was already dead.[55]

Legal standards also provide clear rules and protections for hospitals and those who work in them. In the 1960s, when the first human organ transplants were successfully completed, ethical questions began to arise over when people were technically dead so that their organs could be removed for transplant. Was it enough for the brain to cease electrical activity? What if the heart was still beating (a state that was often required for successful organ harvesting to occur)? These questions ultimately led to a team of doctors and ethicists meeting at Harvard University in 1968 to form the Harvard Brain Death Committee; their goal was to discuss and define exactly what was meant by "dead." The results of this committee's work influenced legislatures in several states, but the definition is still ambiguous in many parts of the country.[56]

Yet for most people who have to deal with end-of-life issues, questions of emancipation and definitions of death seem academic in comparison to the emotional struggles over what to do with loved ones who are unable to communicate. Would they have wanted to go on? Would they have wanted to be hooked up to a machine? What should the family do? To whom should the doctors listen?

Legislatures in many states sought to draft laws with legal standards that allowed the wishes of the incapacitated to be determined in just and equitable ways. Whatever conclusion they arrive at, though, the most important role these laws must serve is to protect the right to life that all people possess, even those in irreversible comas or other permanent vegetative states. Without laws that clearly prove the intent of the patient, hospitals should use all medical action possible to keep their patients alive.

The "clear and convincing evidence" standard is both constitutional and practical.

Throughout the 1980s, attorney William Colby fought for the right of Nancy Cruzan's parents to remove their daughter from life support. Nancy had been in a car wreck in the early 1980s

FROM THE BENCH

Cruzan v. Director, 497 U.S. 261 (1990)

In 1983, Nancy Cruzan suffered a tragic automobile accident and became incapacitated. After Cruzan was diagnosed as being in a persistent vegetative state for at least six years, her parents asked the hospital to remove the feeding tube that was keeping her alive and allow her to die. The hospital refused to do so without a court order, and Cruzan's parents responded by filing one. When the case reached the Supreme Court, it became a landmark for personal liberty regarding medical care:

> We think it self-evident that the interests at stake in the instant proceedings are more substantial, both on an individual and societal level, than those involved in a run-of-the-mine civil dispute ...
>
> We believe that Missouri may permissibly place an increased risk of an erroneous decision on those seeking to terminate an incompetent individual's life-sustaining treatment. An erroneous decision not to terminate results in a maintenance of the status quo; the possibility of subsequent developments such as advancements in medical science, the discovery of new evidence regarding the patient's intent, changes in the law, or simply the unexpected death of the patient despite the administration of life-sustaining treatment at least create the potential that a wrong decision will eventually be corrected or its impact mitigated. An erroneous decision to withdraw life-sustaining treatment, however, is not susceptible of correction.

and was in a persistent vegetative state. Her father asked the hospital to remove her feeding tube, but the hospital refused to do so without a court order. When Nancy's parents asked a judge to order the hospital to remove the tube, the judge refused unless the family could provide "clear and convincing evidence" that Nancy would have wanted to be removed from life support. The judge was unconvinced by the evidence offered, and a legal drama unfolded that caught the attention of a nation.[57]

Central to this legal battle was a Missouri law that required "clear and convincing evidence" that an incapacitated person would want to be removed from life support before such actions occurred. Among the issues the court would look at were the

In sum, we conclude that a State may apply a clear and convincing evidence standard in proceedings where a guardian seeks to discontinue nutrition and hydration of a person diagnosed to be in a persistent vegetative state. We note that many courts which have adopted some sort of substituted judgment procedure in situations like this, whether they limit consideration of evidence to the prior expressed wishes of the incompetent individual, or whether they allow more general proof of what the individual's decision would have been, require a clear and convincing standard of proof for such evidence.

The Supreme Court of Missouri held that in this case the testimony adduced at trial did not amount to clear and convincing proof of the patient's desire to have hydration and nutrition withdrawn. In so doing, it reversed a decision of the Missouri trial court which had found that the evidence 'suggested' Nancy Cruzan would not have desired to continue such measures. . . .

The testimony adduced at trial consisted primarily of Nancy Cruzan's statements made to a housemate about a year before her accident that she would not want to live should she face life as a 'vegetable,' and other observations to the same effect. The observations did not deal in terms with withdrawal of medical treatment or of hydration and nutrition. We cannot say that the Supreme Court of Missouri committed constitutional error in reaching the conclusion that it did.

status of the patient, the quality of her life, the timeliness of the evidence, the closeness of the relatives who testified, and so on. All these factors affected the court's decision in these cases. The Cruzan family argued that such elements should not be required, but that the family's wishes should be respected.[58]

The Supreme Court heard this case in 1989. Writing for the majority of the Court, Chief Justice Rehnquist upheld the Missouri law, finding that the state's clear-and-convincing evidence standard did not violate the U.S. Constitution.[59] Recognizing that under the informed consent doctrine a person does have the right to refuse medical treatment, even food and hydration, in this case,

> such a "right" must be exercised for her, if at all, by some sort of surrogate. Here, Missouri has in effect recognized that under certain circumstances a surrogate may act for the patient in electing to have hydration and nutrition withdrawn in such a way as to cause death, but it has established a procedural safeguard to assure that the action of the surrogate conforms as best it may to the wishes expressed by the patient while competent. Missouri requires that evidence of the incompetent's wishes as to the withdrawal of treatment be proved by clear and convincing evidence. The question, then, is whether the United States Constitution forbids the establishment of this procedural requirement by the State. We hold that it does not.[60]

Clearly, the courts and the medical community are concerned with protecting the rights and lives of those who are most vulnerable, those who cannot speak for themselves. The greatest benefit of this kind of standard is that it protects those who are least able to protect themselves. Although it is assumed that families always look out for the best interest of their members, the reality is that all too often the best interest of the patient is not the highest priority.

Far from attempting to prolong the agony of a family making the hardest of emotional decisions, the "clear and convincing evidence" standard provides benefits for both the family and the hospital. Some may argue that the family's wishes should always be honored, but the reality is that the family is not always in agreement. Legal standards that require greater proof before such life-ending action may be taken provide benefits for the family's emotional well-being. Having to provide proof of a patient's wishes requires the family or guardian to search out and gather proof that will satisfy a court. This proof has the additional benefit of providing proof to the family that they are doing what the patient wants, even if the patient cannot now communicate it.

An additional benefit to the "clear and convincing evidence" standard is that the United States Supreme Court has already found this to be a valid standard, a constitutional requirement that states may place on such important life-ending decisions. With so many elements of the right-to-die discussion lacking clear boundaries or definitions, these heightened standards provide a safe harbor for medical professionals and families.

Advance directives present an opportunity for people to state their intentions.

Opponents of greater legal protections for the incapacitated argue that additional standards merely prolong the suffering of the family and expose a private decision to the unwanted publicity of the courts. Yet advance directives such as living wills or other legally recognized instruments created by patients provide clear proof of a person's intent. Recognizing this reality, many states and the federal government passed legislation requiring hospitals to inform patients about living wills and healthcare planning. The 1991 Patient Self-Determination Act (PSDA) requires hospitals to inform patients of their right to draft advance directives that specifically state their wishes.[61]

Such advanced planning provides an opportunity for those who wish to make a decision to terminate or limit life support and other medical procedures. The option of advance directives also shifts the burden back onto those who want to remove life support; they must prove why the incapacitated individual did not draft a living will earlier. Since this avenue for advanced planning is available, the state should assume that a person without such clear advance directives should have the presumption of life.

Chronology: Right-to-die Jurisprudence

1906 The state of Ohio drafts a bill that would allow physician-assisted suicide (PAS). The bill did not pass, but the idea sparks renewed discussion regarding physicians' roles in the dying process. Also helps spark a debate that includes secular views, religious views, and the state's role in the protection of life.

1967 First modern euthanasia bill is drafted in Florida. It is defeated.

1969 Idaho follows Florida's lead and drafts a similar euthanasia bill. It, too, is defeated, but the trend toward acceptance of PAS is growing.

1976 The court allows Joseph Quinlan, father of the incapacitated Karen Ann Quinlan, to remove her respirator. She breathes independently until her death, 10 years later.

1996 The Supreme Court rules in *Cruzan* that, before an incapacitated adult can be deprived of life-supporting technology, there must be 'clear and convincing evidence' of their personal desire to do so.

1997 Oregon passes the Death With Dignity Act, becoming the first state to allow physician-assisted suicide.

1999 After his video showing him assisting a patient's suicide airs on *60 Minutes,* Dr. Jack Kevorkian is convicted of murder and sentenced to 10 to 25 years in prison.

2005 The Supreme Court orders the removal of Terri Schiavo's feeding tube. She dies 13 days later.

2006 In *Gonzales v. Oregon,* the Supreme Court finds that Oregon's Death With Dignity Act does not violate the Federal Controlled Substances Act because the right-to-die issue belongs to the states, not to the Federal government.

Source: "Chronology of Assisted Dying." Death With Dignity National Center. Available online. URL: http://www.deathwithdignity.org/historyfacts/chronology.asp.

Summary

Given the government's duty to protect life, states act appropriately when they set up standards for determining whether a person should not be put on life support or removing a person from life support. In any important legal situation, legal standards are necessary to avoid abuses and to ensure just actions. Nowhere is this clearer than in those issues involving care for those who are incapacitated. In situations where even the basic definitions of existence, such as when is a person "dead," are in dispute, standards must be put in place.

In its ruling in the *Cruzan* case, the Supreme Court found that Missouri's standard of "clear and convincing evidence" of desire to refuse life support was an appropriate standard for determining whether to remove an incapacitated person from life support. This standard, and others like it, are both constitutional and practical, for they provide a method for acting on a persons wishes, while still protecting the state's interest in safeguarding the life of its citizens. This standard is further supported by laws that allow advance directives to be created that clearly indicate people's preferences if they are ever in a critical situation and difficult decisions must be made.

The State Should Not Intervene to Keep People on Life Support

O ne of the most difficult decisions a family can make is what to do about putting a loved one on life support when the prognosis is not good. This decision is made all the harder when the loved one is suffering and in pain. Should the family prolong the suffering of a loved one? Should they cling to the hope that somehow medicine will find a solution before the loved one expires?

These difficult questions are made all the more difficult when the legal system is involved and interferes in the family's decision making.

The clear and convincing evidence standard Is flawed.

For those who oppose allowing the family to make end-of-life decisions for loved ones without interference from the state, great weight is placed on arguments that additional legal standards protect those who cannot speak for themselves, or who are most prone to abuse. The basis for this argument rests on the assumption that everyone would want to continue their lives, irrelevant of the conditions in which they find themselves. Yet continuing a person's life beyond what he or she would have wanted can result in torture-like medical situations and can limit the autonomy of the patient. The Supreme Court in *Quinlan* has already ruled that people have the right to forego medical treatment and procedures if they wish to die naturally.[62] In *Cruzan*, the Court reaffirmed this right and also pointed out that, just because a person is unconscious, he or she does not lose rights—even the right to die.[63]

One of the biggest problems with the clear and convincing evidence standard is that it requires already distraught families to expose their most private decisions to the scrutiny of open court. In *Quinlan*, the New Jersey Supreme Court recognized that a patient has a liberty interest in the right to privacy, based on U.S. Supreme Court decisions such as *Griswold* (which allowed distribution of birth control based on privacy interests). As the New Jersey court explains,

> The Court in *Griswold* found the unwritten constitutional right of privacy to exist in the penumbra of specific guarantees of the Bill of Rights "formed by emanations from those guarantees that help give them life and substance." Presumably this right is broad enough to encompass a patient's decision to decline medical treatment under certain circumstances, in much the same way as it is broad enough to encompass a woman's decision to terminate pregnancy under certain conditions: *Roe v. Wade*, (1973).[64] (internal citations omitted)

The court also recognized the state did have an interest in protecting the lives of its citizens. The court ultimately decided on a balancing test:

> We think that the State's interest *contra* weakens and the individual's right to privacy grows as the degree of bodily

invasion increases and the prognosis dims. Ultimately there comes a point at which the individual's rights overcome the State interest.[65]

As the court in *Quinlan* points out, medical decisions are one of the most sensitive and private areas that a person has an interest in

Pew Research Center Poll Material

In January of 2006, the Pew Research Center released its findings from an earlier poll questioning American citizens about end-of-life issues. Their results show substantial support for right-to-die issues

- Only 10 percent of those polled disapprove of right-to-die laws, whereas 84 percent support them. The support for such laws has risen 5 percent since 1990.

- 70 percent say there are circumstances in which a patient should be allowed to die.

Among those who believe there are specific circumstances that warrant a patient's choice to die, individual support differs according to those circumstances.

- 60 percent feel that that those who suffer great pain with no hope of improvement should be allowed to die.

- 53 percent limit circumstances to those who have an incurable disease.

- Only 33 percent feel that those who are ready to die because living 'is a burden' should be allowed to do so.

Although there are some who still do not support right-to-die laws, the discussion of end-of-life choices has greatly increased in the last 10 years.

- In 1990, only 71 percent of those polled said they had heard of a living will. In 2005, 95 percent stated that they knew about living wills.

- In 2005, 29 percent of those polled stated that they had a living will, which is a vast increase from the 12 percent who admitted to having a living will in 1990.

keeping private. As such, this area should be provided the greatest respect and protection.

For some scholars, such as Lois Shepherd of Florida State University, the assumption in the law should be shifted. She argued that keeping people alive in a vegetative state, with no ability to sense the world around them in any meaningful way,

- Whether or not respondents had a living will or knew what one was, the poll also showed an increase in those who discussed with their spouse or parents about end-of-life treatment. Only 51 percent had talked with their spouse about end-of-life treatment in 1990, but in the last 15 years, that number increased by almost 20 percent, moving up to 69 percent in 2005.

- The numbers for those who had talked with their mother and father also increased by 14 percent and 20 percent, respectively.

Other findings by the Pew Center also showed the relation between those who have had experience making end-of-life decisions and those who specify their own. For example, people who have made or helped make end-of-life decisions for loved ones are more likely to have a living will or to have discussed the issue with a spouse or close friend. Similarly, more people who have had to make end-of-life decisions for others tend to believe in a moral right to suicide in certain circumstances, and they are not opposed to ending their own medical treatment should an incurable disease or great pain decrease their value of life. In addition, although most support the idea that some circumstances call for the need to cease treatment, fewer of those supporters would wish for personal treatment to be stopped if they were facing a terminal illness. Although the right-to-die debate is still very controversial in America, these findings show that the trend is leaning toward support for the right to die.

Source: "Poll: Strong Public Support for Right to Die." The Pew Research Center for the People and the Press. January 5, 2006. Available online. URL: http://people-press.org/reports/display.php3?ReportID=266

is not done for the benefit of the person in a vegetative state, but is done for the families, politicians, religious leaders, and media who use these situations for their own benefit.

To illustrate, Professor Shepherd pointed to the Terri Schiavo case. Politicians such as then–Senate Majority Leader Bill Frist, a medical doctor from Tennessee, looked at a video segment of Terri and claimed that she was not in a permanent vegetative state. Congress attempted to subpoena Terri Schiavo to appear before a congressional committee in an effort to have her feeding tubes reinserted. While all this was occurring, several wealthy individuals offered millions of dollars to Terri's husband if he would relinquish guardianship and allow Terri's parents to reinsert the feeding tube. The activity surrounding the Schiavo case was meticulously detailed by the ever-present media. Professor Shepherd argued such public spectacles prove that the interests of those involved were not for the patient, but rather to promote their own agenda.[66]

For these reasons, Professor Shepherd argued that the presumption should shift from having to provide "clear and convincing evidence" that a person should be removed from life support, to proving that a person would want to be on life support. As she described it,

> [S]tate law now generally provides that surrogates can decide to discontinue treatment only if they have clear and convincing evidence that such decisions would be a patient's preference or, absent evidence of patient preferences, that such decisions would be in the patient's best interest. In its stead, the law I propose would read that, at a certain time (such as a year) following diagnosis of a patient's permanent vegetative condition, all life-sustaining treatment (including nutrition and hydration) would be terminated unless the surrogate makes a decision in favor of continued treatment on the basis of clear and convincing evidence that continued treatment would be the patient's preference. Gone would be the individ-

ualized best interests analysis out of recognition that patients in a permanent vegetative state uniformly have no present or future interest in living that they can experience. Only if the patient would have wished for continued feeding would it be permitted out of respect for the patient's autonomy. Under this proposed reform, surrogates would not be permitted to authorize the continued feeding of a vegetative patient to further their own or others' interests. The state's role in protecting the patient from being used as an instrument for others takes precedence over the state's interest in sustaining vegetative life.[67]

Whether one agrees with the shifting of presumptions, as Professor Shepherd does, or whether one merely questions the wisdom of state interference in private matters, the heightened level of required proof places unreasonable burdens on suffering families.

Advance directives are unrealistic.

The other major argument for those who oppose allowing the family to make end-of-life decisions unimpeded by the courts is that people can make advance directives that would provide clear and convincing evidence of a person's desired medical treatment if they were to become incapacitated or otherwise unable to make decisions for themselves. This argument is bolstered by the fact that, following the Cruzan case in 1991, Congress passed the Patient Self-Determination Act. This act requires all U.S. hospitals to provide counseling and advice to patients about healthcare planning that includes such end-of-live options as living wills.[68]

The problem with this argument is best seen in the original cases in this area. Karen Quinlan was 22 years old at the time of her accident. Nancy Cruzan was 25 when she was found under her car on the side of the road. Terri Schiavo was 26 when she collapsed in her Florida home. In each of these cases, people in their mid-20s were involved in sudden accidents for which they

Advance Directive

127.531 Form of advance directive. (1) The form of an advance directive executed by an Oregon resident must be the same as the form set forth in this section to be valid. In any place in the form that requires the initials of the principal, any mark by the principal is effective to indicate the principal's intent.

(2) An advance directive shall be in the following form:

...

1. *Close to Death.* If I am close to death and life support would only postpone the moment of my death:

   A. INITIAL ONE:
   ___ I want to receive tube feeding.
   ___ I want tube feeding only as my physician recommends.
   ___ I DO NOT WANT tube feeding.

   B. INITIAL ONE:
   ___ I want any other life support that may apply.
   ___ I want life support only as my physician recommends.
   ___ I want NO life support.

2. *Permanently Unconscious.* If I am unconscious and it is very unlikely that I will ever become conscious again:

   A. INITIAL ONE:
   ___ I want to receive tube feeding.
   ___ I want tube feeding only as my physician recommends.
   ___ I DO NOT WANT tube feeding.

   B. INITIAL ONE:
   ___ I want any other life support that may apply.
   ___ I want life support only as my physician recommends.
   ___ I want NO life support.

3. *Advanced Progressive Illness.* If I have a progressive illness that will be fatal and is in an advanced stage, and I am consistently and permanently unable to communicate by any means, swallow food and water safely, care for myself and recognize my family and other people, and it is very unlikely that my condition will substantially improve:

   A. INITIAL ONE:
   ___ I want to receive tube feeding.
   ___ I want tube feeding only as my physician recommends.
   ___ I DO NOT WANT tube feeding.

B. INITIAL ONE:

___ I want any other life support that may apply.

___ I want life support only as my physician recommends.

___ I want NO life support.

4. *Extraordinary Suffering.* If life support would not help my medical condition and would make me suffer permanent and severe pain:

A. INITIAL ONE:

___ I want to receive tube feeding.

___ I want tube feeding only as my physician recommends.

___ I DO NOT WANT tube feeding.

B. INITIAL ONE:

___ I want any other life support that may apply.

___ I want life support only as my physician recommends.

___ I want NO life support.

5. *General Instruction.*

INITIAL IF THIS APPLIES:

___ I do not want my life to be prolonged by life support. I also do not want tube feeding as life support. I want my doctors to allow me to die naturally if my doctor and another knowledgeable doctor confirm I am in any of the medical conditions listed in Items 1 to 4 above.

. . .

PART D: DECLARATION OF WITNESSES

We declare that the person signing this advance directive:

(a) Is personally known to us or has provided proof of identity;

(b) Signed or acknowledged that person's signature on this advance directive in our presence;

(c) Appears to be of sound mind and not under duress, fraud or undue influence;

(d) Has not appointed either of us as health care representative or alternative representative; and

(e) Is not a patient for whom either of us is attending physician.

. . .

NOTE: One witness must not be a relative (by blood, marriage or adoption) of the person signing this advance directive. That witness must also not be entitled to any portion of the person's estate upon death. That witness must also not own, operate or be employed at a health care facility where the person is a patient or resident.

had not appropriately planned. The reality is that people often fail to plan, especially young people. Although advance directives would certainly make life easier on decision makers during end-of-life controversies, it is unrealistic to assume that young people, who are more likely to survive an accident, plan well enough to prepare advance directives.

Families know best.

Probably the best argument for leaving end-of-life decisions to the family comes from the commonsense argument that no one knows the wishes of a family member better than the family itself. Even the legal system recognizes that family members are the best decision makers, as is seen in the guardianship laws that grant the decision-making role to close family members.

The wisdom of leaving the families to make these decisions is seen most clearly in the *Cruzan* case. Had the family been allowed to make a decision, and had the legal and medical community supported that decision, the grieving family would never have been thrust into the public circus that followed them throughout the trials. For three years, the family fought publicly to have its personal decisions respected. The courts eventually sided with the family, but the amount of needless suffering caused by the delay can never be calculated.

The Cruzans' attorney, William Colby, recounted the closing days of the Cruzan family's time at the center of national attention. For 11 days after the feeding tube was removed, the family kept vigil over Nancy. They were frequently interrupted by protesters, none of whom had even known Nancy or the family. Colby related how, "[I]nside the hospital the family huddled together, day after day, talking softly, holding Nancy's hands, and praying."[69] Outside, protesters like Randall Terry from the pro-life group Operation Rescue played to the cameras and marched in front of the hospital. Just before Christmas, and mere days before Nancy died, protesters placed a sign on the hospital lawn, "Nancy's Gift at Christmas from her Parents and Doctor—DEATH!"[70]

No family should ever have to struggle through end-of-life decisions and the mourning process under these conditions. Yet interference in family decisions such as the requirement of clear and convincing evidence or other heightened legal proof provides the potential for public display and interference in private family matters.

Summary

The state should not intervene in personal family matters, such as when to take someone off life support. Such medical decisions are private, for the family alone to make in consultation with medical professionals, and should not be thrust into the public display of the court system. One of the reasons for keeping these decisions out of the courtroom is the legal standards that are used. Such criteria as clear and convincing evidence of the desire to be removed from life support places the presumption and burden of proof on the family before they make an already difficult decision.

Instead, such presumptions should be shifted away from the family and onto the state, requiring the state to prove that the patients would want to be on life support before forcing them into such treatments. Claims that advance directives, such as living wills, would help alleviate this situation sound good in theory, but as the high profile cases of Quinlan, Cruzan, and Schiavo point out, those who get into these medical conditions are often too young to have thought about end-of-life issues. Finally, the legal system should realize that the family knows best and should stay out of personal matters.

State Bans on Physician- assisted Suicide Protect Life

In 1984, Governor Richard D. Lamm of Colorado told an audience of hospital lawyers that "[E]lderly people who are terminally ill have a 'duty to die and get out of the way' instead of trying to prolong their lives by artificial means."[71] Although Governor Lamm later claimed that the media pulled this comment out of context, these words set off a firestorm of opposition from advocates for the elderly. It also raised in the minds of some the specter of a time when the debate ceases to be about the right to die and becomes a duty to die.

The rancor over Governor Lamm's comments revealed one constant in public opinion throughout the right-to-die debate—the idea that life should be protected. Even those who argue for greater opportunities for physician-assisted suicide or euthanasia tend to agree that life is precious and should be protected in most instances. So, although there are some arguments to be made for increasing right-to-die opportunities, from a practical standpoint, the best reason for continuing state bans on physician-assisted suicide is that they protect life.

If states allow physician-assisted suicide, life will be endangered in three ways: (1) The role of the physician will be confused, both for the physician and the patient. (2) Physician-assisted suicide is the first step toward euthanasia. (3) End-of-life existence will be limited as efforts in palliative care will diminish. (Palliative care is care given to improve the quality of life of patients who have a serious or life-threatening disease.)

Participating in suicide is not ethical medical practice.

One of the most time-honored relationships in modern society is the connection between doctor and patient. Based on the assumption that the doctor is there to heal or otherwise contribute to the patient's health and well-being, patients trust their doctors with their very lives. This is why the American Medical Association (AMA), the largest physicians' group in the country, has listed and physician-assisted suicide, and euthanasia in particular, as a violation of its standards of ethics. As stated in the AMA's ethics code,

> Euthanasia is the administration of a lethal agent by another person to a patient for the purpose of relieving the patient's intolerable and incurable suffering.
>
> It is understandable, though tragic, that some patients in extreme duress—such as those suffering from a terminal, painful, debilitating illness—may come to decide that death is preferable to life. However, permitting physicians to engage in euthanasia would ultimately cause more harm than good. Euthanasia is fundamentally incompatible with the physician's role as healer, would be difficult or impossible to control, and would pose serious societal risks. The involvement of physicians in euthanasia heightens the significance of its ethical prohibition. The physician who performs

euthanasia assumes unique responsibility for the act of ending the patient's life. Euthanasia could also readily be extended to incompetent patients and other vulnerable populations.

Instead of engaging in euthanasia, physicians must aggressively respond to the needs of patients at the end of life. Patients should not be abandoned once it is determined that cure is impossible. Patients near the end of life must continue to receive emotional support, comfort care, adequate pain control, respect for patient autonomy, and good communication. (I, IV) *E-2.21 Euthanasia*[72]

The Story of Terri Schiavo

On a February day in 1990, the peaceful morning hours were shattered when Michael Schiavo found his 26-year-old wife motionless, lying facedown on the floor of their Florida home. After Michael called 911, Theresa Marie (Terri) Schiavo was immediately rushed to a hospital, where doctors discovered that her brain had been without oxygen for almost five minutes after the collapse. They diagnosed her as being in a 'persistent vegetative state,' a state of being in which one can neither think, speak, nor respond to communication, and in which one is unaware of one's surroundings. Although Terri Schiavo could blink and breathe independently, a feeding tube had to be inserted in order for her to receive proper hydration and nutrition.

As weeks and months turned into years, Terri's condition remained the same. In 1992, Michael Schiavo filed a medical malpractice suit on behalf of Terri, and a Florida jury awarded him $300,000 for loss of consortium (defined as the deprivation of spousal benefits due to the defendant's fault). They also awarded Terri Schiavo $700,000, which went in to a trust fund controlled only by her husband.

In 1993, Terri's parents, Robert and Mary Schindler, asked the court to remove Michael and appoint them as Terri's guardians. The court refused, since Florida law clearly maintains that the husband or wife of an incapacitated adult is the sole guardian of that person. The Schindlers' feelings toward Michael Schiavo came from accusations that he was not using the money awarded him in the malpractice suit properly. They claimed that he had neglected to spend any money on

It is also argued, as in J. Gay-Williams essay's "The Wrongful-ness of Euthanasia," that physician-assisted suicide would lead to a decline in the ethics of the medical profession. If medical professionals see their duty as shifting from the saving of lives, to the ending of lives, they may not work as diligently to protect the lives of all their patients. He posits,

> [Euthanasia] could have a corrupting influence so that in any case that is severe doctors and nurses might not try hard enough to save the patient. They might decide that the patient

Terri's recovery, and insisted on keeping her in her current condition rather than helping her recover. Nevertheless, the court upheld the Florida law and allowed Michael to remain as Terri's sole guardian.

Although the dispute between the Schindlers and Michael Schiavo continued, it did not erupt again publicly until 1998, when Michael, claiming that it was Terri's wish, asked the court for permission to remove her feeding tube. The removal would, essentially, deprive Terri of nutrition until she died of starvation. Terri's parents contested this decision, stating that this was never Terri's wish. The court ruled in favor of Michael Schiavo and allowed the tube to be removed.

Two days later, however, the tube was reinserted when the Schindlers filed a civil suit against Michael. After the reinsertion, Michael sought permission for removal a second time. Ultimately, the feeding tube was removed and reinserted a total of three times before the court made its final ruling in 2005 to remove the tube permanently. Despite the uproar from the American public and attempts by the Schindler family to have the feeding tube reinserted, no subsequent court overruled this decision. On March 31, 2005, 13 days after the feeding tube was removed, Terri Schiavo died of malnutrition at the age of 41.

Sources: "Schiavo's Feeding Tube Removed." CNN.com: Law Center. March 18, 2005. Available online. URL: http://www.cnn.com/2005/LAW/03/18/schiavo.brain-damaged/; "Background on the Schiavo Case." CNN.com: Law Center. March 25, 2005. Available online. URL: http://ww.cnn.com/2005/LAW/03/25/schiavo.qa/index.html.

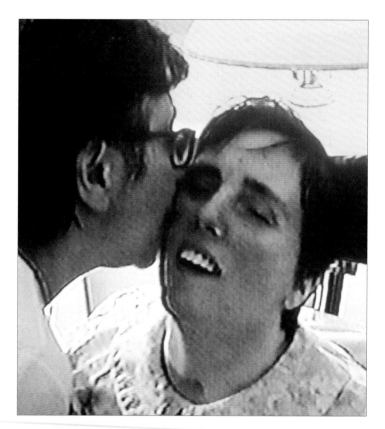

Terri Schiavo (right) gets a kiss from her mother, as shown in this image taken from a videotape in 2001. The conflict over her care between Schiavo's husband and her parents became national news when government officials, including then-governor Jeb Bush, became involved.

would simply be "better off dead" and take the steps necessary to make that come about. This attitude could then carry over to their dealings with patients less seriously ill. The result would be an overall decline in the quality of medical care.[73]

Gay-Williams is not the only one concerned with such "slippery slope" arguments. (Merriam-Webster defines *slippery slope* as "a course of action that seems to lead inevitably from one action or result to another with unintended consequences.") Many others are concerned that the slippery slope will not only end in curtailing physician care, but also could lead to societal changes that encourage a culture of death.

Physician-assisted suicide is a slippery slope to euthanasia.

When dealing with situations of physician-assisted suicide, what may sound merciful and right in the most extreme situation can turn into the standard of care for less extreme cases. This could lead to a permissive state in which not only is physician-assisted suicide allowed, but also other types of euthanasia are permitted eventually. To go from voluntary euthanasia to nonvoluntary euthanasia to involuntary euthanasia would be a steady slide down the slope. Eventually, this could lead to acts of genocide for races or classes of people that do not meet some government requirement or standard. For those who do not think this is a likely trajectory, one has only to look at the slippery slope that occurred in Nazi Germany during Adolph Hitler's rise to power. The people of Germany had no idea where Hitler's programs would eventually lead; had the concentration camps been Hitler's first act, then the people probably would not have supported him. It was only by slowly acclimating the people into a culture of hatred and permissiveness over death that Hitler was able to implement his plans for eugenics and genocide.[74]

Even if physician-assisted suicide does not lead to Hitler's Third Reich or to genocide, it could lead to a culture where the right to die becomes a duty to die. Social Darwinists and utilitarian ethicists have argued that only those that are useful to society should be allowed to survive. Such views may not be expressly stated, but eventually the question will arise as to whose life is worth living, and the decision could be made by society, instead of by the individual. Although this may seem unlikely today, in fewer than 20 years, German culture shifted from an integrated society to a holocaust.

Concerns that society will try to force others into euthanasia is already being addressed by groups like Not Dead Yet. This advocacy group fights against physician-assisted suicide and euthanasia. They point out that, just because someone has a physical limitation, it does not mean he or she fails to contribute to society, or that his or her life is worth any less. On the group's Web site, they explain their beliefs thus:

> People already have the right to refuse unwanted treatment, and suicide is not illegal. What we oppose is a public policy

Senator Bill Frist's Comments on the Senate Floor Regarding the Terri Schiavo Controversy

So then it came to, what do you do? Here is the U.S. Senate that normally does not and should not get involved in all of these private-action cases. It is not our primary responsibility here in the U.S. Senate. But with an exhaustion of a State legislature, an exhaustion of the court system in a State—yet all of this is based on what one judge had decided on what, at least initially, to me, looks like wrong data, incomplete data. But somebody is being condemned to death—somebody who is alive; there is no question she is alive—is being condemned to death...

A single Florida judge ruled that Terri is in this persistent vegetative state. And this is the same judge who has denied new testing, new examinations of Terri by independent and qualified medical professionals. They have not been allowed...

Persistent vegetative state, which is what the court has ruled, I say that I question it, and I question it based on a review of the video footage which I spent an hour or so looking at last night in my office here in the Capitol. And that footage, to me, depicted something very different than persistent vegetative state...

A 1996 British Medical Journal study conducted in England's Royal Hospital for Neurodisability concluded there was a 43 percent error rate in the diagnosis of Persistent Vegetative State. It takes a lot of time, as I mentioned earlier, to make

that singles out individuals for legalized killing based on their health status. This violates the Americans With Disabilities Act, and denies us the equal protection of the law. Some bio-ethicists have even started to argue that intellectually disabled people are not persons under the law. That hasn't happened since slavery was legal.[75]

Their concerns are linked to the realities of managed health care and increasing healthcare costs. They do not want the killing of the disabled to become "just another healthcare option" for those patients who require more medical resources.[76]

this diagnosis with a very high error rate. If you are going to be causing somebody to die with purposeful action, like withdrawal of the feeding tube, you are not going to want to make a mistake in terms of the diagnosis.

I mentioned that Terri's brother told me Terri laughs, smiles, and tries to speak. That doesn't sound like a woman in a persistent vegetative state. So the Senate has acted tonight and the House of Representatives acted last night. The approaches are different, and over the course of tonight and tomorrow, I hope we can resolve those differences. It is clear to me that Congress has a responsibility, since other aspects of government at the State level had failed to address this issue, that we do have a responsibility given the uncertainties that I have outlined over the last few minutes ...

There seems to be insufficient information to conclude that Terry Schiavo is in a persistent vegetative state.

Securing the facts, I believe, is the first and proper step at this juncture. Whoever spends time making the diagnosis with Terri needs to spend enough time to make an appropriate diagnosis. At this juncture, I don't see any justification in removing hydration and nutrition. Prudence and caution and respect for the dignity of life must be the undergirding principles in this case.

Source: Bill Frist Testimony. Congressional Record. 109th Cong., 1st sess., 17 March 2005: S3090 to S3092.

Lifting bans will encourage suicide and limit palliative care.

In 1994, the New York State Task Force on Life and Law released a report called "When Death Is Sought." This group of lawyers, doctors, theologians, and ethicists concluded,

> [We] unanimously recommend that New York laws prohibiting assisted suicide and euthanasia should not be changed. In essence, we propose a clear line for public policies and medical practice between forgoing medical interventions and

Schiavo Relief Act, 109th Cong., 1st sess., 17 March 2005

Be it enacted by the Senate and House of Representatives of the United States of America in Congress assembled,

SECTION 1. RELIEF OF THE PARENTS OF THERESA MARIE SCHIAVO.
The United States District Court for the Middle District of Florida shall have jurisdiction to hear, determine, and render judgment on a suit or claim by or on behalf of Theresa Marie Schiavo for the alleged violation of any right of Theresa Marie Schiavo under the Constitution or laws of the United States relating to the withholding or withdrawal of food, fluids, or medical treatment necessary to sustain her life.

SEC. 2. PROCEDURE.
Any parent of Theresa Marie Schiavo shall have standing to bring a suit under this Act. The suit may be brought against any other person who was a party to State court proceedings relating to the withholding or withdrawal of food, fluids, or medical treatment necessary to sustain the life of Theresa Marie Schiavo, or who may act pursuant to a State court order authorizing or directing the withholding or withdrawal of food, fluids, or medical treatment necessary to sustain her life. In such a suit, the District Court shall determine de novo any claim of a violation of any right of Theresa Marie Schiavo within the scope of this Act, notwithstanding any prior State court determination and regardless of whether such a claim has previously been raised, considered, or decided in State court proceedings. The District Court shall entertain and determine the suit without any delay or abstention

assistance to commit suicide or euthanasia. Decisions to forgo treatment are an integral part of medical practice; the use of many treatments would be inconceivable without the ability to withhold or to stop the treatments in appropriate cases. We have identified the wishes and interests of patients as the primary guideposts for those decisions.[77]

Throughout the report, the task force expressed concerns over the possibility of error and the shift in attention away from palliative care. Palliative care is the area of medical treatment where doctors

---

in favor of State court proceedings, and regardless of whether remedies available in the State courts have been exhausted.

SEC. 3. RELIEF.
After a determination of the merits of a suit brought under this Act, the District Court shall issue such declaratory and injunctive relief as may be necessary to protect the rights of Theresa Marie Schiavo under the Constitution and laws of the United States relating to the withholding or withdrawal of food, fluids, or medical treatment necessary to sustain her life.

...

SEC. 5. NO CHANGE OF SUBSTANTIVE RIGHTS.
Nothing in this Act shall be construed to create substantive rights not otherwise secured by the Constitution and laws of the United States or of the several States.

SEC. 6. NO EFFECT ON ASSISTING SUICIDE.
Nothing in this Act shall be construed to confer additional jurisdiction on any court to consider any claim related—
(1) to assisting suicide, or
(2) a State law regarding assisting suicide.

Source: Schiavo Relief Act, 109th Cong., 1st sess., 17 March 2005. Available at http://thomas. loc.gov/cgi-bin/query/D?c109:3:./temp/~c109gXUWiv::

treat the pain associated with certain medical conditions. This kind of medical assistance is not designed to cure any infirmity, but is instead designed to enhance quality of life in patients. Most groups agree that medical personnel are woefully undertrained in palliative care techniques. The report indicates that there might be more leeway for legalizing physician-assisted suicide in the most extreme cases, but only after advancements have been made in palliative care.[78]

As the report explains, and the 1997 update of the report confirms, the medical community remains concerned about the lack of training and use of palliative care techniques. According to the report, the primary reason that people want a physician's assistance in committing suicide is because of major pain associated with certain incurable ailments. If the medical community could focus on such end-of-life care as pain-alleviating medicines, as well as emotional, spiritual, and intellectual care, then these patients' desire to end life would be reduced.

Summary

Bans on physician-assisted suicide protect the lives of patients by requiring doctors to focus on their primary mission: saving lives. If physician-assisted suicide were allowed, medical care would suffer. The doctor–patient relationship would be harmed, as a patient could no longer trust that his doctor's sole goal was to protect the patient's life. Also, the possibility of error is too great, as the patient may be suffering from depression or other mental problems that could cloud the patient's judgment. Doctors facilitating the deaths of their patients would also start society down a slippery slope that is reminiscent of Nazi Germany and the abuses of the medical community that occurred there. Finally, allowing physician-assisted suicide would encourage suicide by making it a duty, instead of a right, and would hinder advances in palliative care.

State Bans on Physician- assisted Suicide Prolong Suffering

Lonny Shavelson wrote in his book *A Chosen Death: The Dying Confront Assisted Suicide* about his experience with Renee Sahm, a woman with brain cancer, and her struggle over whether to commit suicide. He described her pain and hallucinations, and the disintegration of her body and mind. Shavelson also brings to light some of the struggles people face when they help others with terminal illnesses.

One of these puzzles centered on Sahm's physical capacity to commit suicide, and the paradox that it created. If she were to have the option of physician-assisted suicide, then she could wait longer. She could be assured that suicide would still be a viable option for her if her pain became too great, even if she lost the motor control necessary to accomplish the task unassisted. Because physician-assisted suicide was not an available option, however, she would have to commit suicide earlier, before she lost major motor control.[79]

Such unintended consequences point out the need for laws that allow physician-assisted suicide. Laws validate medical intervention in these situations, allowing terminally ill and possibly handicapped individuals to make their own decisions and retain autonomy. Despite claims by opponents of physician-assisted suicide, such laws would not necessarily lead down a slippery slope to euthanasia or other atrocities. Rather, such laws would provide standards for a practice that already occurs, yet remains unregulated.

Terminally ill people have the right to make their own decisions.

Physician-assisted suicide is ethical and moral because it offers help to those who cannot end their suffering on their own. Some people who are physically impaired because of terminal illness want to end their suffering but are unable to do so because of their disabilities. Denying them physician assistance limits their rights to self-determination.[80]

In their essay "The Role of Autonomy in Choosing Physician Aid in Dying," doctors Thomas Preston, Martin Gunderson, and David Mayo explain:

> Whenever possible, people should be free to determine their fates by their own autonomous choices, especially in connection with private matters, such as health, that primarily involve one's own welfare.... This constitutes what we call the autonomy argument for physician aid in dying.[81]

Arguments countering this assertion, such as the inability of terminally ill patients to make autonomous decisions, ultimately reduce patient autonomy in any situation. As the authors point out, if the terminally ill patient lacks true autonomy because of disease-induced impairments, then how does a critically ill

Oregon's Death With Dignity Act

Oregon residents first voted to enact the Death With Dignity Act (DWDA) in 1994 with 51 percent of the voters in favor of it. The act did not become official, however, until 1997, after a petition was placed on the ballot seeking the repeal of the DWDA . This petition was rejected by an overwhelming 60 percent of Oregon voters, making Oregon the first state to allow physician-assisted suicide (PAS).

The DWDA allows Oregon residents with terminal illnesses to take part in physician-assisted suicide, allowing them to "obtain and use prescriptions from their physicians for self-administered, lethal medications." Although the Death With Dignity Act allows for PAS, it clearly distinguishes PAS from euthanasia. According to the DWDA, euthanasia assumes that the doctor personally injects the medication into the patient, while PAS merely allows the doctors to give patients the prescription or drug rather than personally administering it. Oregon's Death With Dignity Act neither allows nor excuses euthanasia.

The Death With Dignity Act also sets restrictions on the type of patients who can ask for PAS. Only patients who have been diagnosed with a terminal illness by a minimum of two doctors can request physician-assisted suicide. The DWDA thus does not allow for non–terminally ill patients, such as those who are aging or are mentally or physically disabled, to seek PAS.

Once the patient has received multiple diagnoses of terminal illness, they can place a request for physician-assisted suicide. However, when placing this request, they must be deemed capable of making this decision by at least two witnesses, one of whom cannot be family, an inheritor, or the attending physician. The DWDA defines *capable* as "having the ability to make and communicate medical decisions to healthcare providers." This stipulation distinguishes the PAS allowed in the Death With Dignity Act from euthanasia.

After patients have made their first request for PAS, they enter into a 15-day waiting period. If they still seek physician-assisted suicide at the end of the waiting period, lethal medication will be prescribed to them within 48 hours.

Source: Oregon, Death With Dignity Act, Statues (1994) 127.800 §1.01–127.897 §6.01; "Eighth Annual Report on Oregon's Death with Dignity Act." Oregon Department of Human Services. March 9, 2006. Available online. URL: http://www.oregon.gov/DHS/ph/pas/docs/year8.pdf.

patient in need of surgery truly have autonomy to make decisions about treatment?[82] Such arguments lead to negating all
patient decisions about their own care.

Physician-assisted suicide would also help in another
way. Committing suicide is often harder than is commonly
thought. In his book, Shavelson also related an experience
with a man he referred to as Gene, a retired stroke victim who
attempted suicide by cutting his wrists. When that attempt
failed (after intervention the next day by his son), Gene later
tried to poison himself with household chemicals. These two
attempts further limited Gene's capacity for enjoying life and
caused a great deal of pain and suffering. If physician assistance had been made available, Gene would have been able
to follow through with the act without causing himself as
much pain.[83]

Andrew Batavia, in his essay "Disability and Physician
Assisted Suicide," provided broader support for the singular
example just noted. He explained,

> Moreover, some people with major disabilities, such as
> quadriplegia or diseases that severely weaken muscles, sim-
> ply do not have the functional capacity to implement these
> strategies. Others have dysphagia and cannot swallow pills.
> Although it is easy to say that anyone can end his or her life
> independently, the reality is often more complicated, particu-
> larly for people with substantial disabilities.[84]

Allowing physician-assisted suicide does not lead to a slippery slope.

A recurring concern over physician-assisted suicide is that it
is the first step down a slippery slope toward euthanasia and
even genocide. Opponents of physician-assisted suicide often
invoke the specter of Nazi Germany and the medical atrocities
committed by the Third Reich. Noted historian Ian Dowbiggin

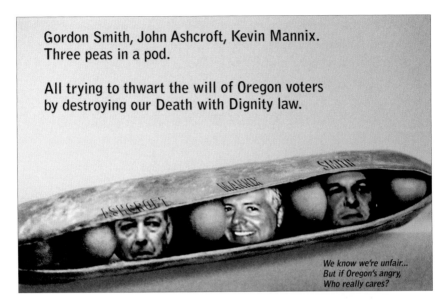

Gordon Smith, John Ashcroft, Kevin Mannix.
Three peas in a pod.

All trying to thwart the will of Oregon voters
by destroying our Death with Dignity law.

*We know we're unfair...
But if Oregon's angry,
Who really cares?*

As the only state in the union to have in place a death-with-dignity act, Oregon has come under close scrutiny. In 2002, Oregon Death With Dignity launched an issue-advocacy campaign lampooning Senate candidate Gordon Smith, gubernatorial candidate Kevin Mannix, and Attorney General John Ashcroft for their criticism of Oregon's law.

cautioned against "playing the Nazi card," as it limits the ability for reasoned debate, resulting instead in emotionally charged invectives that obscure the real issues.[85] Andrew Batvia goes further than Dowbiggin in contrasting the U.S. debate over physician-assisted suicide and the Nazi program of eugenics. As Batvia points out, the Nazis engaged in forced euthanasia of people they felt were impure or defective. These victims were never given the opportunity to choose their fate. The U.S. debate over physician-assisted suicide is not about allowing the state to impose euthanasia on the unwilling, but is instead about the right of the individual to make decisions without the interference of the state. The political reality is also different; Nazi Germany was run by an all-powerful state in which the government often made decisions for the individual. The U.S. debate over physician-assisted suicide focuses instead on the freedom of the individual to make decisions for himself.[86] As Dowbiggin sums up, "[N]ot every slope is slippery, and not all medical abuse is tantamount to Nazism."[87]

Moving from the theoretical to the real world, the United States' limited experience with state-condoned physician-assisted suicide is confined to the state of Oregon. Because of the rigorous review and data collection related to the Oregon law, the reality seems to show that even when physician-assisted suicide is a legal option, it is rarely chosen. Even those who oppose physician-assisted suicide, such as conservative author David E. Lee from the Hastings Center, conceded,

> Finally, it is significant that the Oregon experience to date in no way suggests that a slide down a slippery slope is imminent. The option allowed by Oregon's Death With Dignity Act has been used very sparingly. In 2001 (the most recent year for which statistics are available as this article goes to press), 21 Oregonians chose to end their lives by ingesting a lethal dose of medication prescribed by a physician, accounting for 0.33 percent of the 6,365 Oregon deaths from similar diseases. During 2000, the number was 27 (0.38 percent) of the 6,964 deaths from similar diseases. The number of Oregonians opting for physician-assisted suicide has remained fairly stable, ranging from 16 in 1998, the first year the law was in effect, to 27 in both 1999 and 2000. Clearly, there is no landslide in the making.[88]

In much the same way that the United States is not similar to Nazi Germany, so our program in physician-assisted suicide is not like that of the Netherlands, where doctors actively engage in the suicide process, injecting the drugs themselves. In Oregon's program, the doctor may provide the medicine, but it is up to the patient to actually ingest the drugs.[89]

Strict regulation has advantages over allowing the practice to remain unregulated.

For those who wish to prevent physician-assisted suicide from moving from voluntary to some form of involuntary or non-voluntary euthanasia, legalization may be the best way to avoid the slide down the slippery slope. It is common knowledge in the medical field that physicians already assist some patients in committing suicide. This may occur in different ways, from allowing the patient access to too many drugs to actively inject-ing the patients with an overdose. Although medical-interest groups such as the American Medical Association claim to stand against physician-assisted suicide, they have done nothing to stop it from occurring, even when they are clearly aware of its occurrence. This creates a culture of lawlessness, where illegal actions are taking place, and no laws are in effect to make sure that suicide is truly the wish of the patient.[90]

The literature is filled with stories not only of doctors, but also of family members and loved ones who succumbed to the pleas of suffering patients and ended their lives. Laws have not stopped those intent on making such a final decision, nor have they stopped those willing to run the risk of criminal action to help the people they care for. Legalization of assisted suicide would allow for state regulation and avoid additional trauma and suffering (from failed attempts, etc.). It also leaves loved ones with the choice of helping those who cannot help themselves. Such laws would eliminate the risk of families having to engage in criminal action to alleviate the suffering of a loved one.[91]

Legalization would also bring to light the practices that are occurring, thus allowing those who seek suicide a fuller understanding of the practice. Such understanding would allow patients to make better, more informed decisions. It would also allow for more humane methods of suicide as practices are evaluated in a scientifically reviewed environment.

Finally, despite what some people may claim, a physician's job is not always to save lives. In reality, not every life can be saved. In those instances, a doctor's role is to provide comfort and dignity in the process of dying. For those who have a future with no comfort or dignity left, a physician is fulfilling his or her highest calling by easing the inevitable death. This

Sample Oregon Form

Oregon Revised Statute 127.897 s.6.01. Form of the request.
A request for a medication as authorized by ORS 127.800 to 127.897 shall be in substantially the following form:

REQUEST FOR MEDICATION TO END MY LIFE IN A HUMANE
AND DIGNIFIED MANNER

I, _____, am an adult of sound mind.

    I am suffering from _____, which my attending physician has determined is a terminal disease and which has been medically confirmed by a consulting physician.

    I have been fully informed of my diagnosis, prognosis, the nature of medication to be prescribed and potential associated risks, the expected result, and the feasible alternatives, including comfort care, hospice care, and pain control.

    I request that my attending physician prescribe medication that will end my life in a humane and dignified manner.

INITIAL ONE:

    _____ I have informed my family of my decision and taken their opinions into consideration.

    _____ I have decided not to inform my family of my decision.

    _____ I have no family to inform of my decision.

I understand that I have the right to rescind this request at any time.

    I understand the full import of this request and I expect to die when I take the medication to be prescribed. I further understand that although most deaths

also allows the dying patient the dignity and autonomy of picking the time and manner of death, thus allowing friends and family to be a part of this most intimate, and ultimately inevitable, activity.

---

occur within three hours, my death may take longer and my physician has counseled me about this possibility.

I make this request voluntarily and without reservation, and I accept full moral responsibility for my actions.

Signed: _____

Dated: _____

DECLARATION OF WITNESSES

We declare that the person signing this request:

(a) Is personally known to us or has provided proof of identity;

(b) Signed this request in our presence;

(c) Appears to be of sound mind and not under duress, fraud, or undue influence;

(d) Is not a patient for whom either of us is attending physician.

_____ Witness 1/Date

_____ Witness 2/Date

NOTE: One witness shall not be a relative (by blood, marriage, or adoption) of the person signing this request, shall not be entitled to any portion of the person's estate upon death and shall not own, operate or be employed at a healthcare facility where the person is a patient or resident. If the patient is an inpatient at a health care facility, one of the witnesses shall be an individual designated by the facility.

Summary

Bans on physician-assisted suicide needlessly prolong the suffering of patients and therefore should be overturned. These bans limit the ability of the most severely disabled people and those patients who are suffering the most from exercising their right to stop their suffering. By disallowing physician-assisted suicide, those who cannot end their own lives, or do not know how, are limited in their autonomy. Those who claim that allowing physician-assisted suicide leads down a slippery slope to euthanasia or atrocities similar to those perpetuated by Hitler's Nazi regime do not recognize the broad differences between the political realities of Nazi Germany and democracy in the United States.

Finally, legalizing physician-assisted suicide would merely provide structure for a practice that is already occurring, but is unregulated. Because of a lack of regulation and oversight, there is no guarantee that patients' wishes are being respected or that best practices are being used in the current situation.

The Future of the Euthanasia Debate

In June 2007, Dr. Jack Kevorkian is scheduled to be paroled from the prison sentence he began serving in April 1999.[92] This slight, 78-year-old man with oversized glasses hardly seems the controversial firebrand who rekindled a debate that continues to divide the nation.

The right-to-die debate is not likely to subside anytime soon. After the Schiavo controversy played out in the media, interest groups on both sides of the issue were energized to take up the debate that had momentarily fallen from public view. Major issues that continue to drive controversy include:

- What role should state and federal governments play in the dispute?

- What is the physician's role and what should it be?

- Where is the line between suicide and euthanasia, and why?

What Role Should Federal and State Governments Play?

One area of continued controversy will occur between states and the federal government in determining how physician-assisted suicide laws and other right-to-die provisions that begin to turn up in states should be handled. This controversy was highlighted in 2006, when the Supreme Court found that doctors in the state of Oregon could continue to abide by the Death With Dignity Act without fear of losing their licenses.[93]

The Oregon controversy began in 2001, when then–Attorney General John Ashcroft added interpretive language to

---

FROM THE BENCH

Gonzales v. Oregon

Four years after the state of Oregon passed its Death With Dignity Act (DWDA), the Attorney General of the United States added an interpretive rule to the federal Controlled Substances Act (CSA) stating that physician-assisted suicide does not constitute a legitimate medical purpose, and any physician who prescribes lethal drugs will have their medical license either suspended or revoked. This rule of the Controlled Substances Act directly contradicted the Oregon Death With Dignity Act because the ODWDA stated that physicians who abided by the stipulations of ODWDA would not be in danger of losing their license in any way.

The state of Oregon and some of its residents challenged the new interpretive rule of the CSA, and the Supreme Court ultimately found in favor of the state of Oregon. In the court's opinion, Justice Kennedy stated that because regulation of medical practices is typically reserved for the states, Oregon's state-enacted law takes higher priority than the federal rule, and so the attorney general cannot revoke their license so long as they stay within the bounds of Oregon's Death With Dignity Act. Justice Kennedy wrote:

Even though regulation of health and safety is "primarily, and historically, a matter of local concern," there is no question that the Federal Government

the federal Controlled Substances Act (CSA). This act was originally intended to provide a national response to drug trafficking, but Attorney General Ashcroft added an interpretive rule that would suspend or revoke the medical license of any physician who prescribed lethal drugs as part of a physician-assisted suicide. As this had the effect of practically invalidating the 1997 Oregon law allowing physician-assisted suicide, the state sued to have the provision overturned. Oregon claimed that this change in interpretation went beyond what Congress intended and interfered with the right of the state to regulate the practice of medicine.[94] The controversy ultimately arrived at the Supreme Court, where Justice Kennedy wrote the majority opinion of the divided Court. He concluded,

can set uniform national standards in these areas. In connection to the CSA, however, we find only one area in which Congress set general, uniform standards of medical practice.

This provision strengthens the understanding of the CSA as a statute combating recreational drug abuse, and also indicates that when Congress wants to regulate medical practice in the given scheme, it does so by explicit language in the statute.

For all these reasons, we conclude the CSA's prescription requirement does not authorize the Attorney General to bar dispensing controlled substances for assisted suicide in the face of a state medical regime permitting such conduct.

The Government, in the end, maintains that the prescription requirement delegates to a single Executive officer the power to affect a radical shift of authority from the States to the Federal Government to define general standards of medical practice in every locality. The text and structure of the CSA show that Congress did not have this far-reaching intent to alter the federal–state balance and the congressional role in maintaining it.

Source: *Gonzales v. Oregon*, 126 S. Ct. 904 (2006).

The [federal] Government, in the end, maintains that the prescription requirement delegates to a single Executive officer the power to effect a radical shift of authority from the States to the Federal Government to define general standards of medical practice in every locality. The text and structure of the CSA show that Congress did not have this far-reaching intent to alter the federal-state balance and the congressional role in maintaining it.[95]

By denying the attorney general the right to make this interpretive change, the Court confined these types of decisions about medical practice within the realm of the state governments. This is important for reasons of federalism. Federalism is the system of government where power is divided between the national government and the states. Controversy surrounds this concept in the United States because of the struggle between the national government and the states over the power to make laws regarding different issues. The Gonzales case demonstrates a push by the U.S. attorney general toward increased federal powers over areas that were once solely the purview of the state. Coupled with other federalism controversies, such as education or marriage, *Gonzales* indicates that such federalism battles are not over. The involvement of members of Congress in the Schiavo controversy further indicates that this area will see more court controversies.

What Role Should a Physician Play?

Another area of continued future controversy in the right-to-die debate will remain focused on the appropriate role of the physician. For some, a physician's sole responsibility is to save lives. Any deviation from that goal is considered contrary to the sanctity of the profession. Others view the physician's role as lifesaver, but argue that, when a life cannot be saved, or when the patient wishes for life to end, the physician should respect those decisions and instead do what is possible to make the

Protesters in wheelchairs, many wearing "Not Dead Yet" t-shirts, demonstrate outside of Dr. Jack Kevorkian's home in 1996, during Kevorkian's third trial for assisted suicide. Not Dead Yet is an advocacy group that opposes the legalization of assisted suicide.

patient comfortable. Some people have also raised concerns over what will be required of physicians as the law changes. If a physician is allowed to assist in a suicide, could it some day happen that physicians are required to assist in suicides (by prescribing lethal doses of drugs, etc.) if the patient demands it?[96]

Although the legal parameters are already set by state and federal laws, changes in these laws will reinvigorate the debate about this controversy. Oregon might have been the first state to redefine the role of the physician with its Death With Dignity Act, but it will likely not be the last.

What is the difference between suicide and euthanasia?

Dr. Kevorkian's invention of his Thanatron increased confusion about whether he was assisting suicides or whether he was actively involved in euthanizing patients. The Thanatron,

Dr. Jack Kevorkian

Jack Kevorkian was born and raised in Pontiac, Michigan. After receiving his undergraduate and medical degrees from the University of Michigan, he became licensed to practice medicine in 1952. Kevorkian's specialty was pathology, a field of medicine which seeks to determine causes of death and disease. During his residency, Dr. Kevorkian was dubbed "Dr. Death," because of an odd obsession with the dead and the dying. (As a resident, he asked to take the night shift because more people died at night.)

After more than 20 years as a resident doctor in Michigan, Kevorkian moved to California to pursue a career in film production. After his first attempts at directing failed, he remained in California, practicing as a pathologist. He wrote many articles on euthanasia; these were published in little known medical journals. Kevorkian later returned to Michigan but was unable to find a job because of his writings. During this time, Kevorkian traveled to Amsterdam, where he witnessed several assisted suicides.

On his return to Michigan, Kevorkian placed advertisements in magazines and journals for terminally ill patients, offering help to those who desired to die. Although very few responded at first, eventually word of Kevorkian's methods became widespread, and he gained publicity as "Dr. Death." Kevorkian was charged with murder at least three times but was never convicted because his patients pushed a button on his *Thanatron* (Greek for "death machine") in order to end their own life—he never officially took part in their deaths and was therefore not legally held to blame.

In November 1998, CBS's *60 Minutes* aired a tape given to them by Dr. Kevorkian, which showed him assisting a suicide. America watched in shock as a Michigan resident suffering from Lou Gehrig's disease, 52-year-old Thomas Youk, received a lethal injection from Dr. Kevorkian. Kevorkian told those involved with *60 Minutes* that he wanted to use this videotape not merely to create the public controversy that would ensue, but also to change the debate from one centered on the legal-

his "suicide machine," was designed by Dr. Kevorkian out of household items and parts available at home and garden stores. It involved the use of three liquids and a timer. Once hooked up to the machine intravenously (by IV), the patient could pull the

ity of "physician-assisted suicide" to one centered on "euthanasia." Kevorkian stated that he wanted the authorities to make a final decision on whether or not euthanasia should be legalized.

Michigan authorities stated that they wanted to view the entire tape before charging Dr. Kevorkian, perhaps because they knew that his multiple acquittals were based on the fact that he never directly administered drugs to a patient he was assisting. The difference in the Youk case, however, was that Kevorkian administered the drugs by his own hand, rather than allowing the patient to do so.

As a result of the broadcast, Michigan authorities arrested Dr. Kevorkian and charged him with assisting a suicide and administering a controlled substance. Although the charges for assisting a suicide were dropped, the court found him guilty of murder through administering a controlled substance and sentenced him to 10 to 25 years in prison. After 7 years in prison and two failed parole attempts, Kevorkian is set to be paroled in the summer of 2007 because of his degenerating health. (Kevorkian is suffering from multiple ailments, including osteoporosis and hepatitis C.)

Although the *60 Minutes* segment resulted in Kevorkian's imprisonment, it had the positive effect of regenerating debates about the medical and moral ramifications of physician-assisted suicide and euthanasia. Throughout the United States, debate has ensued among proponents of euthanasia and their opposition, and although euthanasia is still illegal in all 50 states, its legalization is significantly more of a possibility than it was before the Kevorkian controversy.

Source: "Death Watch." PBS's *Online NewsHour*. November 24, 1998. Available online. URL: http://www.pbs.org/newshour/bb/media/july-dec98/suicide_11-24.html; "Dr. Kevorkian and Physician Assisted Suicide: History and Facts." *Creighton University School of Medicine*. Available online. URL: http://medicine.creighton.edu/idc135/2004/Group4a/history.htm; "Lawyer: Kevorkian May Die Before '07 Parole." *Foxnews. com*, November 19, 2005. Available online. URL: http://www.foxnews.com/story/0,2933,176127,00.html.

trigger and start the flow of drugs into his or her system.[97] For some observers, this seemed to allow the autonomy to remain with the patient, but for others, this kind of advanced involvement with the death makes the physician who inserts the needle into the patient guilty of euthanasia.

For some doctors, this distinction is as meaningless as is the belief that not starting life support is a valid choice, but once a patient is on such support, it is wrong to remove it. Professor Andrew Batavia sees little practical difference between these kinds of actions, preferring instead to look at the desires and autonomous decisions of the patient. In his eyes, once the patient makes the decision, the implementation of that decision is purely mechanical, whether it is ingesting a drug on one's own or having a doctor inject it. This is particularly true for those patients who are disabled to the point that they could not commit suicide without assistance.[98] Others, such as members of Not Dead Yet and other advocacy groups, sharply disagree.[99]

As time progresses and legal definitions become more precise, the line between suicide and euthanasia will become increasingly problematic. Is it euthanasia if the doctor puts the drugs in the needle for the patient? What if the doctor puts the needle in the vein, but the patient pushes the plunger? How far is too far when it comes to "helping" with a suicide?

Summary

The controversy over the right to die is not likely to be resolved anytime soon. Although some issues, such as the right to refuse care and the right to commit suicide, have been laid to rest by court decisions and laws, other issues will take their place. In particular, the relationship between the state and federal governments is ever changing, and, through this change, federal intervention in areas traditionally controlled by states could change the right-to-die debate, particularly when it involves physician-assisted suicide. The role of those physicians in relation to their patients is also likely to change with time. Finally, the level of action involved in the process of death could blur the lines between who is assisting in a suicide and who is actively euthanizing a patient.

NOTES ///////

Introduction: History of the Euthanasia Debate

1 "Kevorkian Furthers Controversy with Euthanasia Tape." *CNN.com*. November 22, 1998. Available online. URL: http://www.cnn.com/US/9811/22/kevorkian/index.html?eref=sitesearch; James, Caryn, "Critic's Notebook: '60 Minutes,' Kevorkian, and a Death for the Cameras." *The New York Times*. November 23, 1998. Available online. URL: http://query.nytimes.com/gst/fullpage.html?sec=health&res=9E0CE5DC1E30F930A157 52C1A96E958260.

2 "Hippocratic Oath: Classical Version." PBS's *NOVA Online*. Available online. URL: http://www.pbs.org/wgbh/nova/doctors/oath_classical.html.

3 The modern version of the oath does not include this language. It has been modified to focus more on general principles than specific rules. Modern medical ethicists inserted these changes after arguing that the classic prohibitions were as anachronistic as the original introductory paean to the gods[0], particularly those portions that prohibit relations with patients, etc. See http://www.pbs.org/wgbh/nova/doctors/oath_today.html.

4 "History of Euthanasia." *Euthanasia.com*. Available online. URL: http://www.euthanasia.com/historyeuthanasia.html.

5 Ian Dowbiggin, *A Concise History of Euthanasia*. Oxford: Rowman & Littlefield, 2005, pp. 42–44.

6 Ibid., pp. 52–60; "Chronology of Assisted Dying." *Death With Dignity National Center*. Available online. URL: http://www.deathwithdignity.org/historyfacts/chronology.asp.

7 Dowbiggin, *Concise History*, pp. 82–84.

8 Ibid., pp. 124–125; Ian Dowbiggin, *A Merciful End: The Euthanasia Movement in Modern America*. New York: Oxford University Press, 2003, p. 144.

9 *In re Quinlan*, 70 N.J. 10 (1976): 27.

10 Ibid., pp. 55–56.

11 Dowbiggin, *A Merciful End*, p. 146.

12 William H. Colby, *Unplugged: Reclaiming Our Right to Die in America*. New York: AMACOM, American Management Association, 2006, pp. 80–82.

13 *Cruzan v. Director*, 497 U.S. 261 (1990), 266–270.

14 Ibid.

15 Ibid.

16 Garner, Bryan A., ed. *Black's Law Dictionary*. 7th ed. (St. Paul, Minn.: West Group, 1999) 577.

17 Ibid.

18 Ibid., pp. 278, 280.

19 Ibid.

20 "Prosecutor: Tape Seems to Show Homicide." *The Michigan Daily*. November 24, 1998. Available online. URL: http://www.pub.umich.edu/daily/1998/nov/11-24-98/news/news12.html.

21 Raphael Cohen-Almagor, *The Right to Die With Dignity: An Argument in Ethics, Medicine, and Law*. Chapel Hill, N.C.: Rutgers University Press, 2001, pp. 192–199.

22 "Assisted Suicide Advocate to be Paroled in June." *CNN.com*. December 13, 2006. Available online. URL: http://www.cnn.com/2006/law/12/13/kervorkian.parole ap/index.html.

23 Colby, *Unplugged*, pp.12–18.

24 Ibid., p. 40.

25 Ibid., p. 45.

26 Bryan A. Garner, ed. *Black's Law Dictionary*, 7th ed. St. Paul, Minn.: West Group, 1999, p. 575.

27 Oregon Death With Dignity Act, ORS 127.800

28 Quill, Timothy E., and Margaret P. Battin. *Physician Assisted Dying: The Case for Palliative Care and Patient Choice*. New York: Johns Hopkins University Press, 2004, pp. 70–71.

Point: States Have a Duty to Protect Life in All Forms

29 The Declaration of Independence. Available online. URL: http://www.ushistory.org/declaration/document/index.htm.

30 Plato. *Laws, Book IX.* Available online. URL: http://www.classicallibrary.org/ plato/dialogues/laws/book9.htm.

31 Aristotle. *Nicomachean Ethics.* Available online. URL: http://classics.mit.edu/ Aristotle/nicomachaen.5.v.html.

32 Thomas Hobbs. *Leviathan,* XIII. Available online. URL: http://oregonstate.edu/ instruct/phl302/texts/hobbes/leviathan-c .html.

33 William E. Phipps, "Christian Perspectives on Suicide," *The Christian Century* (October 30, 1985): pp. 970–972.

34 "Declaration on Euthanasia." *Sacred Congregation for the Doctrine of Faith,* May 5, 1980. Available online. URL: http://www.vatican.va/roman_curia/ congregations/cfaith/.

35 Resolution 6. *Southern Baptist Convention Annual Meeting.* Available online. URL: http://www.sbcannualmeeting .org/sbc01/sbcresolution.asp?ID=6.

36 Steven H. Resnicoff, "Physician-assisted Suicide Under Jewish Law." *Jewish Law Articles,* 1998. Available online. URL: http://www.jlaw.com/articles/ phys-suicide.html.

37 Qu'ran Surrahs 4:29,17:33. Available online. URL: http://www.submission.org.

38 "Buddhism, Euthanasia, and Suicide." BBC's *Religion & Ethics* Web page. Available online. URL: http://www.bbc .co.uk/religion/religions/buddhism/ buddhistethics/euthanasiasuicide.shtml.

39 "When Death Is Sought: Assisted Suicide and Euthanasia in the Medical Context, Chapter 5." *Task Force on Life and the Law, New York State Department of Health's Web Page.* Available online. URL: http://www.health.state.ny.us/nysdoh/ consumer/patient/chap5.htm.

40 Ibid., p. 90.

41 "Euthanasia, E-2.21." *American Medical Association's Code of Ethics.* August 22, 2006. Available online. URL: http://www .ama-assn.org/ama/pub/category/8458 .html.

42 "Poll: Strong Public Support for Right to Die." *The Pew Research Center for the People and the Press,* 5 January 2006. http://people-press.org/reports/display .php3?ReportID=266.

43 *Cruzan v. Director,* 497 U.S. 261 (1990): p. 282.

Counterpoint: End-of-life Decisions Are Personal Matters

44 "Patrick Henry's Give Me Liberty or Give Me Death! Speech." The University of Oklahoma: College of *Law's A Chronology of U.S. Historical Documents* page. Available online. URL: http://www.law .ou.edu/ushistory/henry.shtml.

45 *Cruzan v. Director,* 497 U.S. 261 (1990).

46 U.S. Constitution, Amendment 14.

47 *In re Quinlan,* 70 N.J. 10 (1976).

48 "2005 California HealthCare Foundation and the Health Privacy Project Poll." *Electronic Privacy Information Center.* Available online. URL: http://www.epic .org/privacy/medical/polls.html.

49 *Griswold v. Connecticut,* 381 U. S. 479 (1965).

50 *Roe v. Wade,* 410 U.S. 113 (1973).

51 *Lawrence v. Texas,* 539 U.S. 558 (2003).

52 "Privacy and Your Health Information." Office of Civil Rights-HIPAA, *United States Department of Health and Human Services* Web page. Available online. URL: http://www.hhs.gov/ocr/hipaa/ consumer_summary.pdf.

Point: Without Clear Evidence of Intent, Life Support Should Be Administered

53 Colby, *Unplugged,* pp. 12–13.

54 Ibid., pp. 78–80.

55 Ibid.

56 Ibid.

57 *Cruzan v. Director,* 497 U.S. 261 (1990): pp. 266–270.

58 Ibid.

59 Ibid., p. 281.

60 Ibid.

61 Cohen-Almagor, *The Right to Die With Dignity,* p. 32.

Counterpoint: The State Should Not Intervene to Keep People on Life Support

62 *In re Quinlan*, 70 N.J. 10 (1976).

63 *Cruzan v. Director*, 497 U.S. 261 (1990).

64 *In re Quinlan*, 70 N.J. 10 (1976), p. 41.

65 Ibid., p. 42.

66 Lois Shepherd. "In Respect of People Living in a Permanent Vegetative State—and Allowing Them to Die." *16 Health Matrix: Journal of Law-Medicine* 631 (Summer 2006): pp. 632–635.

67 Ibid., pp. 676–677.

68 Dowbiggin, *A Merciful End*, pp. 168–169.

69 Colby, *Unplugged*, p. 93.

70 Ibid.

Point: State Bans on Physician-assisted Suicide Protect Life

71 "Gov. Lamm Asserts Elderly, If Very Ill, Have 'Duty to Die.'" *New York Times.* (March 29, 1984). Available online. URL: http://query.nytimes.com/gst/fullpage.html?sec=health&res=9E01E5D91E39F93AA15750C0A962948260.

72 "Euthanasia, E-2.21." *American Medical Association's Code of Ethics.* August 22, 2006. Available online. URL: http://www.ama-assn.org/ama/pub/category/8458.html.

73 J. Gay-Williams, "The Wrongfulness of Euthanasia" (1979), in Ronald Munson, ed., *Intervention and Reflection: Basic Issues in Medical Ethics*, 5th ed. Wadsworth, 1996: pp. 168–171. Available online. URL: http://spot.colorado.edu/~heathwoo/Phil164/gay-williams.pdf.

74 Dowbiggin, *Concise History*, pp. 91–99.

75 Not Dead Yet's "About" Web page. *Notdeadyet.org.* Available online. URL: http://www.notdeadyet.org/docs/about.html.

76 Ibid.

77 "When Death Is Sought: Assisted Suicide and Euthanasia in the Medical Context, Chapter 5." *Task Force on Life and the Law, New York State Department of Health's* Web page. Available online. URL: http://www.health.state.ny.us/nysdoh/consumer/patient/chap5.htm.

78 Ibid.

Counterpoint: State Bans on Physician-assisted Suicide Prolong Suffering

79 Lonny Shavelson, *A Chosen Death: The Dying Confront Assisted Suicide.* New York: Simon & Schuster, 1995, p. 28.

80 Dowbiggin, *A Merciful End*, pp. 154–155.

81 Thomas Preston, Martin Gunderson, and David J. Mayo. "The Role of Autonomy in Choosing Physician Aid in Dying," in T. E. Quill and M. P. Battin, eds. *Physician Assisted Dying: The Case for Palliative Care and Patient Choice.* New York: Johns Hopkins University Press, 2004, p. 39.

82 Ibid., p. 42.

83 Shavelson, *A Chosen Death*, pp. 99–102.

84 Andrew Batavia, "Disability and Physician-assisted Dying," in Quill and Battin, *Physician Assisted Dying*, p. 68.

85 Dowbiggin, *A Merciful End*, p. xiv.

86 Batavia, p. 64.

87 Dowbiggin, *A Merciful End*, p. xiv.

88 Daniel E. Lee, "Physician-assisted Suicide: A Conservative Critique of Intervention," *The Hastings Center Report.* January 1, 2003. Available online. URL: http://www.deathwithdignity.org/news/news/hastings.01.03.asp.

89 Oregon, *Death With Dignity Act, Statutes* (1994) 127.800 §1.01–127.897 §6.01.

90 Charles H. Baron, "The Seven Deadly Sins of the Status Quo," in Quill and Battin, *Physician Assisted Dying*, pp. 314–315.

91 Ibid.

Conclusion: The Future of the Euthanasia Debate

92 "Assisted Suicide Advocate to be Paroled in June." *CNN.com.* December 13, 2006. Available online. URL: http://www.cnn.com/2006/law/12/13/kervorkian.parole.ap/index.html.

93 *Gonzales v. Oregon*, 126 S. Ct. 904 (2006).

94 Ibid.

95 Ibid., p. 926.

96 Ed Newman, "Part Five: Making the Final Choice: Should Physician-Assisted Suicide Be Legal," *Ethical Issues in Terminal Health Care.* Available online. URL: http://www.cptelecom.net/~ennyman/DAS-5.html.

97 "The Thanatron." PBS's *The Kevorkian Verdict* Web page. Available online. URL: http://www.pbs.org/wgbh/pages/ frontline/kevorkian/aboutk/ thanatronblurb.html.

98 Batvia, *Physician-assisted Dying*, pp. 70–71.

99 Not Dead Yet's "About" Web page. *Notdeadyet.org.* Available online. URL: http://www.notdeadyet.org/docs/about .html.

RESOURCES //|||//

Books

Cohen-Almagor, Raphael. *The Right to Die With Dignity: An Argument in Ethics, Medicine, and Law.* Chapel Hill, N.C.: Rutgers University Press, 2001.

Colby, William H. *Unplugged: Reclaiming Our Right to Die in America.* New York: AMACOM, American Management Association, 2006.

Dowbiggin, Ian. *A Concise History of Euthanasia: Life, Death, God, and Medicine.* Oxford, U.K.: Rowman & Littlefield, 2005.

Dowbiggin, Ian. *A Merciful End: The Euthanasia Movement in Modern America.* New York: Oxford University Press, 2003.

Foley, Kathleen M., and Herbert Hendin. *The Case Against Assisted Suicide: For the Right to End of Life Care.* New York: Johns Hopkins University Press, 2004.

Kaufman, Sharon R. *. . . And A Time to Die: How American Hospitals Shape the End of Life.* New York: Scribner, 2005.

Quill, Timothy E., and Margaret P. Battin. *Physician Assisted Dying: The Case for Palliative Care and Patient Choice.* New York: The Johns Hopkins University Press, 2004.

Shavelson, Lonny. *A Chosen Death: The Dying Confront Assisted Suicide.* New York: Simon & Schuster, 1995.

Miscellaneous

Bill Frist Testimony. Congressional Record, March 17, 2005: S3090 to S3092.

"CBS's Assisted Suicide Decision," Transcript: PBS *NewsHour* broadcast, November 24, 1998. Available online. URL: http://www.pbs.org/ newshour/bb/media/july-dec98/suicide_11-24.html.

"Right to Die? Legal, Ethical, and Public Policy Implications." Transcript, May 6, 2005. The Pew Forum on Religion and Public Life. Available online. URL: http://pewforum.org/events/index.php?EventID=73.

"Taking Care: Ethical Caregiving in Our Aging Society." The President's Council on Bioethics, September 2005. Available online. URL: http:// www.bioethics.gov/reports/taking_care/index.html.

Web Sites
Pro-euthanasia Organizations
Compassion & Choices

www.compassionandchoices.org
Formed in January 2005, this organization began by uniting Compassion in Dying and End-of-Life Choices, two euthanasia-advocate groups. It seeks to reform laws that limit patients' ability to choose the way in which they die.

Death With Dignity National Center

www.deathwithdignity.org
Both nonpartisan and nonprofit, this organization led to the education and legal defense of Oregon's Death With Dignity Act. In addition to the extensive defense of the Oregon law, this organization also takes part in lobbying and coalition building in order to respond to political challenges.

Euthanasia Research and Guidance Organization

www.finalexit.org
This nonprofit organization seeks to educate the terminally ill and others on end-of-life decisions by improving the quality of research about physician-assisted suicide and euthanasia. It also performs research and generates briefs for journalists, authors, and other right-to-die organizations.

Anti-euthanasia Organizations
Disability Rights Education and Defense Fund (DREDF)

www.dredf.org
Founded in 1979, DREDF is a leading national civil rights law and policy center under the leadership of people with disabilities and parents of children with disabilities. It seeks to advance the civil and human rights of people with disabilities, including end-of-life decisions.

International Task Force on Euthanasia and Assisted Suicide

www.internationaltaskforce.org
Through networking, educational resources, media relations, and other methods of communication, this organization seeks to ensure that patients receive care and compassion rather than be pressured into assisted suicide.

Nightingale Alliance

www.nightingalealliance.org
Through education of the public, this organization promotes natural death rather than death through unnatural means and at an unnatural time.

Not Dead Yet

www.notdeadyet.org
Founded in April 1996, this organization opposes physician-assisted suicides and euthanasia, claiming that they discriminate against the mentally or physically disabled. This organization communicates through trial testimony, political action, and lobbying in multiple countries.

Cases and Statutes

In Re Quinlan, 70 N.J. 10 (1976)

The Court upheld the right of Joseph Quinlan to take his daughter, a woman who was diagnosed as being in a persistent vegetative state, off her respirator. In this case, the Supreme Court first mentioned an individual's "right to die."

Cruzan v. Director, Missouri Department of Health, 497 U.S. 261 (1990)

In this decision, the court allowed Nancy Cruzan's parents to remove her feeding tube. In this case, the Supreme Court created the clear and convincing evidence standard that must be met before an incapacitated person could be taken off life support.

Theresa Maria Schindler Schiavo, ex. Rel. Robert Schindler and Mary Schindler v. Michael Schiavo, guardian, 403 F. 3d 1289 (2005)

In this landmark decision, the circuit court ruled that Michael Schiavo, as Terri Schiavo's official guardian, could legally have her feeding tube removed despite great opposition from Terri's parents and the public.

Gonzales, Attorney General v. Oregon, 126 S. Ct. 904 (2006)

This decision held that the attorney general of the United States could not make an interpretive rule making illegal certain acts that Oregon's Death With Dignity Act legalized. The Court ruled that because medicine has always been state regulated, no federal authority can create a rule declaring otherwise, notwithstanding a state law.

Oregon Death With Dignity Act, Oregon Law 127.800 (1997)

This Oregon statute legalized physician-assisted suicide in the state of Oregon. Although it continued to outlaw euthanasia after making a clear distinction between it and physician assisted suicide, the bill proved to be very controversial and still comes under public scrutiny and criticism.

Terms and Concepts

advance directive

autonomy

clear and convincing evidence

Controlled Substances Act

eugenics

euthanasia

Fourteenth Amendment

genocide

guardian ad litem

Health Insurance Portability and
Accountability Act

involuntary euthanasia

living will

nonvoluntary euthanasia

Oregon Death With Dignity Act

palliative care

physician-assisted suicide

right to die

right to privacy

slippery slope

suicide

terminal illness

Thanatron

voluntary euthanasia

Beginning Legal Research

The goal of Point/Counterpoint is not only to provide the reader with an introduction to a controversial issue affecting society, but also to encourage the reader to explore the issue more fully. This appendix, then, is meant to serve as a guide to the reader in researching the current state of the law as well as exploring some of the public-policy arguments as to why existing laws should be changed or new laws are needed.

Like many types of research, legal research has become much faster and more accessible with the invention of the Internet. This appendix discusses some of the best starting points, but of course "surfing the Net" will uncover endless additional sources of information—some more reliable than others. Some important sources of law are not yet available on the Internet, but these can generally be found at the larger public and university libraries. Librarians usually are happy to point patrons in the right direction.

The most important source of law in the United States is the Constitution. Originally enacted in 1787, the Constitution outlines the structure of our federal government and sets limits on the types of laws that the federal government and state governments can pass. Through the centuries, a number of amendments have been added to or changed in the Constitution, most notably the first ten amendments, known collectively as the Bill of Rights, which guarantee important civil liberties. Each state also has its own constitution, many of which are similar to the U.S. Constitution. It is important to be familiar with the U.S. Constitution because so many of our laws are affected by its requirements. State constitutions often provide protections of individual rights that are even stronger than those set forth in the U.S. Constitution.

Within the guidelines of the U.S. Constitution, Congress—both the House of Representatives and the Senate—passes bills that are either vetoed or signed into law by the President. After the passage of the law, it becomes part of the United States Code, which is the official compilation of federal laws. The state legislatures use a similar process, in which bills become law when signed by the state's governor. Each state has its own official set of laws, some of which are published by the state and some of which are published by commercial publishers. The U.S. Code and the state codes are an important source of legal research; generally, legislators make efforts to make the language of the law as clear as possible.

However, reading the text of a federal or state law generally provides only part of the picture. In the American system of government, after the legislature passes laws and the executive (U.S. President or state governor) signs them, it is up to the judicial branch of the government, the court system, to interpret the laws and decide whether they violate any provision of the Constitution. At the state level, each state's supreme court has the ultimate authority in determining what a law means and whether or not it violates the state constitution. However, the federal courts—headed by the U.S. Supreme Court—can review state laws and court decisions to determine whether they violate federal laws or the U.S. Constitution. For example, a state court may find that a particular criminal law is valid under the state's constitution, but a federal court may then review the state court's decision and determine that the law is invalid under the U.S. Constitution.

It is important, then, to read court decisions when doing legal research. The Constitution uses language that is intentionally very general—for example, prohibiting "unreasonable searches and seizures" by the police—and court cases often provide more guidance. For example, the U.S. Supreme Court's 2001 decision in *Kyllo* v. *United States* held that scanning the outside of a person's house using a heat sensor to determine whether the person is growing marijuana is unreasonable—*if* it is done without a search warrant secured from a judge. Supreme Court decisions provide the most definitive explanation of the law of the land, and it is therefore important to include these in research. Often, when the Supreme Court has not decided a case on a particular issue, a decision by a federal appeals court or a state supreme court can provide guidance; but just as laws and constitutions can vary from state to state, so can federal courts be split on a particular interpretation of federal law or the U.S. Constitution. For example, federal appeals courts in Louisiana and California may reach opposite conclusions in similar cases.

Lawyers and courts refer to statutes and court decisions through a formal system of citations. Use of these citations reveals which court made the decision (or which legislature passed the statute) and when and enables the reader to locate the statute or court case quickly in a law library. For example, the legendary Supreme Court case *Brown* v. *Board of Education* has the legal citation 347 U.S. 483 (1954). At a law library, this 1954 decision can be found on page 483 of volume 347 of the U.S. Reports, the official collection of the Supreme Court's decisions. Citations can also be helpful in locating court cases on the Internet.

Understanding the current state of the law leads only to a partial under-standing of the issues covered by the POINT/COUNTERPOINT series. For a fuller understanding of the issues, it is necessary to look at public-policy argu-ments that the current state of the law is not adequately addressing the issue.

Many groups lobby for new legislation or changes to existing legislation; the National Rifle Association (NRA), for example, lobbies Congress and the state legislatures constantly to make existing gun control laws less restrictive and not to pass additional laws. The NRA and other groups dedicated to various causes might also intervene in pending court cases: a group such as Planned Parenthood might file a brief *amicus curiae* (as "a friend of the court") — called an "amicus brief" — in a lawsuit that could affect abortion rights. Interest groups also use the media to influence public opinion, issuing press releases and frequently appearing in interviews on news programs and talk shows. The books in POINT/COUNTERPOINT list some of the interest groups that are active in the issue at hand, but in each case there are countless other groups working at the local, state, and national levels. It is important to read everything with a critical eye, for sometimes interest groups present information in a way that can be read only to their advantage. The informed reader must always look for bias.

Finding sources of legal information on the Internet is relatively simple thanks to "portal" sites such as FindLaw (*www.findlaw.com*), which provides access to a variety of constitutions, statutes, court opinions, law review articles, news articles, and other resources — including all Supreme Court decisions issued since 1893. Other useful sources of information include the U.S. Government Printing Office (*www.gpo.gov*), which contains a complete copy of the U.S. Code, and the Library of Congress's THOMAS system (*thomas.loc.gov*), which offers access to bills pending before Congress as well as recently passed laws. Of course, the Internet changes every second of every day, so it is best to do some independent searching. Most cases, studies, and opinions that are cited or referred to in public debate can be found online — and *everything* can be found in one library or another.

The Internet can provide a basic understanding of most important legal issues, but not all sources can be found there. To find some documents it is necessary to visit the law library of a university or a public law library; some cities have public law libraries, and many library systems keep legal documents at the main branch. On the following page are some common citation forms.

COMMON CITATION FORMS

Source of Law	Sample Citation	Notes
U.S. Supreme Court	*Employment Division* v. *Smith*, 485 U.S. 660 (1988)	The U.S. Reports is the official record of Supreme Court decisions. There is also an unofficial Supreme Court ("S. Ct.") reporter.
U.S. Court of Appeals	*United States* v. *Lambert*, 695 F.2d 536 (11th Cir.1983)	Appellate cases appear in the Federal Reporter, designated by "F." The 11th Circuit has jurisdiction in Alabama, Florida, and Georgia.
U.S. District Court	*Carillon Importers, Ltd.* v. *Frank Pesce Group, Inc.*, 913 F.Supp. 1559 (S.D.Fla.1996)	Federal trial-level decisions are reported in the Federal Supplement ("F. Supp."). Some states have multiple federal districts; this case originated in the Southern District of Florida.
U.S. Code	Thomas Jefferson Commemoration Commission Act, 36 U.S.C., §149 (2002)	Sometimes the popular names of legislation—names with which the public may be familiar—are included with the U.S. Code citation.
State Supreme Court	*Sterling* v. *Cupp*, 290 Ore. 611, 614, 625 P.2d 123, 126 (1981)	The Oregon Supreme Court decision is reported in both the state's reporter and the Pacific regional reporter.
State Statute	Pennsylvania Abortion Control Act of 1982, 18 Pa. Cons. Stat. 3203-3220 (1990)	States use many different citation formats for their statutes.

107

PICTURE CREDITS ///|||//

JOHN E. FERGUSON Jr., M.T.S., J.D., is the Deputy Director of the Academy of Freedom Honors program and Assistant Professor of Political Science at Howard Payne University in Brownwood, Texas. He earned his undergraduate degree from Howard Payne University and his M.T.S. and J.D. degrees from Vanderbilt University's Divinity and Law Schools. He is a member of the bar in Tennessee and Washington, D.C. Prior to his academic career, Mr. Ferguson worked for the First Amendment Center in Nashville, Tennessee, as a First Amendment Education coordinator. He consults nationally with school districts, helping them deal with First Amendment issues. He is also an academic consultant for a number of publishers.

ALAN MARZILLI, M.A., J.D., lives in Washington, D.C., and is a program associate with Advocates for Human Potential, Inc., a research and consulting firm based in Sudbury, Massachusetts, and Albany, New York. He primarily works on developing training and educational materials for agencies of the federal government on topics such as housing, mental health policy, employment, and transportation. He has spoken on mental health issues in 30 states, the District of Columbia, and Puerto Rico; his work has included training mental health administrators, nonprofit management and staff, and people with mental illnesses and their families on a wide variety of topics, including effective advocacy, community-based mental health services, and housing. He has written several handbooks and training curricula that are used nationally and as far away as the territory of Guam. He managed statewide and national mental health advocacy programs and worked for several public interest lobbying organizations while studying law at Georgetown University. He has written more than a dozen books, including numerous titles in the Point/Counterpoint series.